WEIR

SIMON & SCHUSTER

New York London Toronto Sydney

COOKING

IN THE CITY

More Than 125 Recipes and Inspiring Ideas
for Relaxed Entertaining

■ ■ ■

JOANNE WEIR

PHOTOGRAPHS BY PENINA MEISELS

SIMON & SCHUSTER
Rockefeller Center
1230 Avenue of the Americas
New York, NY 10020

For information about special discounts for bulk purchases,
please contact Simon & Schuster Special Sales:
1-800-456-6798 or business@simonandschuster.com

Designed by Laura Lindgren

Manufactured in the United States of America

10 9 8 7 6 5 4 3 2 1

Library of Congress Cataloging-in-Publication Data

Weir, Joanne.
Weir cooking in the city : more than 125 recipes and inspiring ideas for relaxed entertaining /
Joanne Weir ; photographs by Penina Meisels.
p. cm.
Includes index.
1. Cookery, International. I. Title: Cooking in the city. II. Title.
TX725.A1.W37523 2004
641.59—dc22
2003067192

ISBN 0-7432-4663-2

To the great cities of the world and the people who make them so . . .

CONTENTS

Preface: City! 15

The Essential City Pantry 19

Entertaining in the City 23

The Right Wine 35

Firsts

Salads

Soups

Mains and a Few Sides

Desserts

WEIR COOKING IN THE CITY

City!

don't think there's ever been a better time to live in a city. In just about every
neighborhood, you can find dozens of interesting restaurants, gourmet food markets, farmers' markets and outdoor stalls selling seasonal produce, artisanal bakeries
and cheese makers, and little shops stocked with shelves of amazing ethnic food
specialties.

Don't think I have anything against small towns. I grew up in one and my mother
would kill me if I said anything bad about our life there. In my books *Weir Cooking,
Recipes from the Wine Country,* and *Joanne Weir's More Cooking in the Wine Country,* I
write reverently about life in a pastoral California valley (where they just happen to
make some of the best wines in the world, but still . . .).

Cities are where most of us live and something amazing is happening in them.
New restaurants and markets are stocked with ingredients from all over the world;
grocery shelves strain under the weight of specialty oils and vinegars; bins overflow
with exotic grains and spices and dizzying arrays of fresh produce, breads, and meats.

Not surprisingly, our level of sophistication about ingredients, food, and wine is at
an astonishing level. Our friends, our kids, for heaven's sake, know so much now about
food. (I was in a supermarket delicatessen recently and watched a preschool-aged

girl point at the dolmas and sushi with as much familiarity as I might have a peanut butter and jelly sandwich a generation ago.)

In the small New England town where I grew up, our choice of ethnic food was Chinese or pizza (and it wasn't very good at that), and the most unusual ingredient you could get at the market was, say, pickled herring. Nobody under the age of thirty will even believe that you couldn't buy coffee beans at the market then!

But all this sophistication comes at a price, and I think most of us would like things to be simpler, slower, easier. Wouldn't you like to be able to make food with a lot of style but without so much effort; to have friends over for dinner without having to plan it too many days in advance; to be able to entertain spontaneously for once; to be able to spend a whole day making something special and then leisurely enjoy it with people you care about?

I can help. You don't need more stuff to do. I can show you where to go and what to do to make fresh, delicious meals for every season and occasion. I'll give you ideas about how to talk to the fishmonger or butcher to get the best cut of meat or the freshest seafood. I'll show you how to pick the best wine for a dish or how to make the dish fit a favorite wine; how to incorporate specialty foods and how to put your own twist on ethnic recipes; how to entertain with greater ease and pleasure.

It all starts with learning to use the amazing cities we live in to their fullest. As I've traveled and cooked my way through many of the world's greatest cities, from Boston to Seattle to the cities along the Mediterranean and through Italy and France, I've learned to see the resources of the city much as a forager might, full of small treasures that are almost as much pleasure to seek as to find.

In San Francisco, where I live, I found one of the finest bakeries in the city just a few blocks from my house, and not much farther, a small, family-owned shop where I can buy the highest-quality meats and fish. Downtown, there is the new, permanent farmers' market where I can buy the very best produce from local organic farmers.

I can wander into Chinatown to my favorite place for Shanghai noodles and then into one of the tiny, crowded markets around the corner to buy all the ingredients to make my own at home. In the Italian neighborhood of North Beach, I found a bakery that sells fresh focaccia so now I can make my own panini. And in the Mission, I came across a produce stand selling the most beautiful Mexican limes and bouquets of cilantro for a dollar, and fresh plantains and plum tomatoes for a song.

When I make these trips through my city and into some of the neighborhoods that have been transforming themselves into mini food meccas, it's as though there is music playing in the streets. It's a city infatuated with food. As Julia Child said, "Who wouldn't become ravenous in such a place?"

But so it is everywhere. In my work as a teacher, I travel all over America and the world. I've seen it. Yeah, we're cooking in the city! This book honors all the amazing things that have been happening with food and the people all over this globe who are making our cities places where great food is being created and enjoyed and the differences between us are being celebrated and savored.

Most of you probably don't remember that old TV show that opened, "There are eight million stories in the naked city. This is just one of them." Well, I'm just one person, but millions of you are creating this incredible time in the life of cities. This is your book. Enjoy!

—Joanne Weir

San Francisco

Spring 2004

The Essential Mediterranean Pantry

On the shelves

Anchovy fillets

Beans and legumes
  *chickpeas, cannellini beans, fava beans,
  French lentils*

Breads
  focaccia, pita bread

Capers

Chocolate

Dried porcini mushrooms

Grains
  bulgur, couscous, farro, polenta, semolina

Honey

Nuts
  *almonds, hazelnuts, pine nuts, pistachios,
  walnuts*

Oils
  extra-virgin olive oil, walnut oil

Olives
  Kalamata, Lucque, Niçoise, Picholine

Pasta

Phyllo dough

Rice

Spices
  *allspice, black pepper, cardamom, cayenne
  pepper, cinnamon, coriander, crushed red
  pepper, cumin, fennel seeds, ginger, sweet
  paprika, saffron, turmeric*

Tahini or sesame paste

Tapenade

Tomato products
  *canned tomatoes, sun-dried tomatoes,
  tomato paste*

Tuna in olive oil

Vinegars
  *balsamic vinegar, red wine vinegar, sherry
  vinegar, white wine vinegar*

In the refrigerator

Cheeses
  *feta, Gorgonzola, manchego, mozzarella,
  Parmigiano-Reggiano, ricotta, Roquefort*

Fresh herbs
  basil, oregano, parsley, rosemary, thyme

Fresh vegetables and fruits

bell peppers, eggplant, garlic, lemons,
onions, tomatoes

The Essential Latin Pantry

On the shelves

Beans
  black beans (canned and dried), garbanzo beans (canned), pinto beans (canned and dried), refried beans (canned)

Chicken stock

Chiles
  Canned or fresh: serrano chiles
  Dried, whole and powdered: ancho, cayenne, chipotle, jalapeño, pasilla

Chocolate, Mexican sweet

Corn oil

Grains
  barley, quinoa, wheat

Herbs and spices
  bay leaves, coriander seeds, cumin, dried marjoram, Mexican cinnamon, Mexican oregano, red chile powder, saffron

Masa harina

Mole

Pumpkin seeds

Rice

Salsa

Tomatillos and tomatoes, canned

Wine vinegar

In the refrigerator

Chorizo sausage

Cilantro

Ezpazote, fresh

Masa, fresh

Queso fresco (Mexican white cheese)

Tortillas (corn and flour)

Fresh vegetables and fruits

avocado, corn (white, yellow, black, and purple), garlic, limes, peppers (Anaheim, bell), tomatillos, tomatoes

The Essential Asian Pantry

On the shelves

Chapati flour

Coconut milk

Cornstarch

Dashi powder

Mushrooms, dried black or shiitake

Oils
 chili oil, peanut oil, sesame oil

Panko (Japanese bread crumbs)

Rice wine vinegar

Sauces and seasoning pastes
 black bean sauce, chili paste (also known as hot chili sauce), Chinese hot mustard, fish sauce, garlic chili sauce, hoisin sauce, oyster sauce, satay sauce, soy sauce, tamari, Thai green and red curry pastes

Spices
 cardamom, Chinese five-spice powder, coriander, cumin, fennel, saffron, szechuan peppercorn, turmeric

Wakame, dried

Wasabi

Wine

Chinese rice wine or dry sherry, mirin, sake

In the refrigerator or freezer

Kaffir lime leaves

Miso

Noodles
 bean thread noodles, Chinese egg noodles, ramen noodles, rice noodles, soba, somen, udon

Rice
 long-grain, basmati, and jasmine rice

Wrappers
 egg roll wrappers, wonton wrappers

Vegetables

bamboo shoots, bean sprouts, bok choy, cilantro, ginger, Japanese eggplant, lemon grass, mushrooms (fresh and wood ears), napa cabbage, Thai sweet basil, water chestnuts

Stop By for a Bite

I remember when the two words *impromptu entertaining* used to fill me with dread. (The scenarios: My brother drops into the city and wants to stop by for dinner. My agent calls and has to meet with me this afternoon at my house. I go to the movies with a group of friends and they all want to come home with me for a late supper.)

Over the years, though, I've learned to apply the same careful planning to these impromptu gatherings as I do to formal entertaining. Now, impromptu is probably the way I entertain most frequently and most pleasurably. This is more how it happens now: I go to the farmers' market and see the most beautiful tomatoes and nectarines; on the way home, I call a couple of friends and invite them to lunch or dinner that night.

Here are a few of the ways I make it all work:

1. I keep my freezer stocked with homemade soup; pizza dough; cookie dough (I especially like icebox cookies); and crisp topping (to sprinkle on seasonal fruit, which I almost always have around, for an instant fruit dessert).
2. I keep several good cheeses on hand in my refrigerator (one soft; one hard; and some Parmigiano-Reggiano).

3. In my pantry in airtight containers, I keep good quality crackers, cookies (like biscotti), dried pasta, and chocolate.

4. For drinks, I keep bottled water on hand (sparkling and still), tea, and, of course, plenty of white and red wine, champagne, and Prosecco.

5. I know that I can always make bruschetta. I start with some good bread, which I always have on hand; toast it using a grill, broiler, or toaster; rub it with a clove of garlic; brush it with extra-virgin olive oil; and sprinkle it with salt. My guests are thrilled.

6. And when all else fails, I remember what my grandmother used to say, "Tis a gift to be able to make soup out of a stone." I practice that gift quite often. The more I play with what I have on hand, the better I get.

Come By After the Theater

A soup party is an easy way to entertain, especially if you're going to be out for the evening with friends at a play or movie, and you want to get together for a simple meal, either before or after. I can get virtually everything ready ahead of time and then just heat the soups (I like to serve a few) at the last minute.

If I am serving dinner after an outing, I set out everything I can before I go: bowls (I like to use small round soup bowls on a large plate); napkins; spoons and knives; and the cheeses and breads, covered with plastic. When we return, I take the soups out of the refrigerator and warm them up while people help themselves to wine, bread, and cheese. Sometimes I serve the soup; other times, I just have guests serve themselves with a ladle straight from the soup pot as they're ready.

One of my favorite menus includes three pots of soup (one pureed; one broth-based with lots of stuff in it; and one that's almost a stew, maybe with grains, for the person dying for something more substantial); an assortment of three to four cheeses; and breads (grainy rustic bread, olive or walnut bread, or homemade corn muffins). Or I might serve one soup, followed by a special salad and dessert.

Tapas and Tango

A party built around small plates can be a perfect way to entertain in the city. It's informal, it gets people involved by letting them create their own meal, and the food can be infinitely interesting. Your menu can be as simple as a few olives or shavings of manchego cheese (a sheep's milk cheese from Spain) or as elaborate as empanadas (the meat and potato turnovers from Spain) and a tortilla espagnole. You can make a whole dinner of small plates or they can be just a little something with drinks before going out. I find that it isn't necessary to finish with an elaborate dessert, but I might put out a simple cookie or a bite of chocolate.

A party of small plates is a lot like an old-fashioned cocktail party, with the emphasis shifted from the drinks to the food. You could even say its roots date back to the invention of tapas, the Spanish small plates, in the *tascas,* or taverns, of a century ago. At that time, a smart bartender thought of putting a top or plate (*tapar* means "to cover") over customers' wine glasses to prevent the fruit flies from falling in. Then the bartender got really smart and realized that if he or she put something salty, almonds, anchovies, or olives, on the plate, they'd sell more wine.

When I'm planning my menu for a Party of Small Plates, I like to put together a mix of hot and room-temperature plates, and to include something doughy, something vegetable-based, something with cheese, and something with meat. I include a throw-in-the-pan item (like shrimp with garlic and sherry) or a toss-on-the-grill dish (like skewers of tuna or chicken). And I serve bread with a dipping sauce or puree, like Romesco (a quintessential Spanish blend of ground almonds, peppers, tomatoes, and olive oil).

MENU FOR A PARTY OF SMALL PLATES

Moroccan Shellfish Cigars (page 81)
Smoked Eggplant with Pita Chips (page 55)
Dried Plums Stuffed with Gorgonzola and Walnuts (page 68)
Prosciutto, Parmigiano, and Pepper Breadsticks (page 60)
A platter of prosciutto, salami, or capocollo with olives, pickled
    vegetables, and roasted peppers

I like to have most of the dishes made ahead, but since it's fun to involve your guests, I leave some dishes to prepare at the last minute, and put a couple of my guests to work chopping or stirring.

I don't put everything out at the beginning. I usually set out a few plates to start on a low table, and then set out the more substantial ones on a larger table that can accommodate those guests who wish to talk and be seated.

And don't forget the music. Maybe some tango.

Aperitivo

I never serve drinks without a little plate of something to eat, nor do I serve a first course without drinks. But just what to serve . . . ?

There is always a good dry martini and of course white wine—a good Sauvignon Blanc, Chardonnay, or Pinot Grigio—or a red, like Pinot Noir, that is light, refreshing, and not too demanding. I also love to serve a glass of Prosecco, a naturally sparkling wine from Northern Italy; cava, a Spanish sparkling wine; or sherry, say, a fino, amontillado, or manzanilla.

I'm never without champagne (sometimes I'll add a splash of cassis for a Kir), or a California sparkling wine. And I'm a fan of Bellinis (page 315), Prosecco combined with fresh white peach, pear, or cherry juice, depending on the season. And during the winter months, I'll substitute freshly squeezed pomegranate juice.

Getting to the Table on Time

Cooking for guests can be intimidating, especially when you're trying to synchronize several dishes. And though it probably sounds obvious to tell you that the solution is good planning and preparation, if you're making more complicated dishes, it's the only way to do it. There isn't a single professional chef, including me, who would even think of trying to pull off a complex meal without detailed, advance planning; prepping, partially cooking, or making absolutely everything that one can ahead of time; and leaving just the assembly for last. It's second nature to us.

PLANNING

Carefully think through your menu and the individual recipes several days in advance, but preferably up to a week ahead. Don't pick recipes that require a lot of last-minute attention (like risotto or a soufflé) or that are extremely complicated (save these for another time); *do* pick recipes that you've mastered; and if you're a beginning cook, don't plan more than one difficult or lengthy recipe per meal.

Decide what time you'll serve the first course, the main, and the dessert. Write down the times on an index card with any other key instructions and put it up somewhere where you'll be able to see it easily. Decide which plates, dishes, and serving pieces you will use for each course, and determine whether there is special equipment you need to buy. Read through each recipe at least once before you make it; what are the cooking techniques and times? And remember to allow yourself *extra* time. Set a goal for yourself to have everything done one hour before guests arrive.

PREPARATION

Almost any dish can be put together, started, or partially cooked ahead of time. Wet and dry ingredients for pastry, breads, or cakes can be combined in separate bowls the day before cooking and mixed together the next day; soups can be completed the day or a couple of days before; everything for salads and vegetables can be prepped ahead of time; spices, herbs, and garnishes can be chopped or sliced and set aside in small bowls; virtually all desserts can be made ahead (don't pick one that can't).

So You Want to Make It Ahead?

BLANCHING

One of my favorite tricks with vegetables is to blanch them first and then warm them just before serving. For example, in the spring I might blanch sugar snap peas, asparagus, English peas, and fava beans, then shock them in ice water and put them aside. When I'm ready, I put a little olive oil in a sauté pan and warm them all together, adding salt and freshly ground pepper to taste.

BRAISING

Braised dishes are perfect for entertaining: they benefit from being prepared ahead of time and are often easy on the budget as well. The meat turns out incredibly juicy and tender (my favorite part), and the sauce is made right in the pot, which is why I always use some good homemade stock. You simply reheat a braised dish shortly before serving (my other favorite part).

GRILLING

I love grilling—both for the flavor and the ease. I get my marinade, relish, and sauces done ahead of time, and all that remains is to cook the meat. In most cases, I serve the relish or sauce at room temperature.

FIVE GREAT MAKE-AHEAD MAIN DISHES

Spiced Lamb Sausage with French Lentils (page 240)

Green Lasagne with Artichokes and Leeks (page 200)

Oven-Baked Penne with Wild Mushrooms and Fontina (page 197)

Spaghetti with Meatballs (page 192)

Braised Chicken with Green Garlic (page 177)

B.Y.O.A. Party (Bring Your Own Apron Party)

There will always be a place for the formal dinner party, but more and more I really like parties that involve my guests. My favorite is what I call the Hands-On Party, because my guests participate in preparing the dinner.

The simplest way to do this (and the one I recommend if you have a small, city kitchen) is to have everyone bring a small first course of their choosing and you make the main course and dessert.

The other way to do a hands-on party involves guests at a whole other level. I plan the menu, do all the shopping and some of the prep, and *they* do all of the cooking (as I run around and help). It can be a little chaotic at first, but if you can get through the initial chaos, it's really fun. At the end, everybody goes home with a copy of the recipes and, I hope, great memories.

Here is a basic plan if you want to try it.

BEFORE THE PARTY

* Think about how many people your kitchen will accommodate. As a guide, my large and open kitchen, which was designed for teaching and filming, can accommodate twelve people.
* Plan the menu: I like to organize the menu around a theme. I've tried all of the following with great success: Midnight Moroccan Fest; Italian Dinner from the Trattoria; Greek Dinner at the Taverna; Tapas and Meze; Mexican Salsa Party; Dim Sum Buffet; or a Sushi Party.
* Go through your kitchen to make sure you have everything in the way of equipment (have extra aprons on hand in case someone forgets one). I have plenty of knives, but you might ask your guests to bring their favorite chef's knife.
* Hire a person to help serve and handle the cleanup so you and your guests can relax.
* Make copies of the recipes, one set per guest.
* Shop for all of the ingredients.

THE DAY OF THE PARTY

Before people arrive, get everything set up. Put out the ingredients for each recipe on its own tray. If you have extra time, wash and spin the salad greens, pick parsley, and chop onions. I always prep all of the ingredients for the dessert, especially if it's baked, since the measurements need to be exact.

* Have all of the guests arrive at the same time and give them all a glass of wine or bubbly. Give them an apron (or have them put their own on) and a copy of the recipes, and then gather everybody at the table.

* Assign people to a recipe (I like to have two to three people working on each recipe) and tell each group what they'll be making. Have everyone read through their recipe. Tell everyone the timetable (first course served at such and such a time, for example) so they can synchronize their efforts.

* Give a short tour of your kitchen: open drawers so everyone will know where spoons and measuring cups are; show them the knife and pan racks. Sometimes I'll give a few tips, like the technique for cutting up a chicken or forming ravioli.

* Everybody cooks for the next hour or so, except you. Your job is to oversee everything, make sure the timetable is followed, and answer questions as they arise.

* When the cooking is done, the cooks become guests again and sit at the table while you and the server finish and garnish the dishes and bring the food to the table.

WHAT SHOULD WE HAVE FOR DINNER?
(MY DOS AND DON'TS FOR MENU PLANNING)

1. I try not to duplicate ingredients. If I start with Crostini with Gorgonzola, I won't serve Risotto with Gorgonzola; or if I start with a cherry tomato pizza, I won't serve a main-course chicken with tomatoes.

2. I try not to duplicate techniques. I won't do a first-course soufflé and then a dessert soufflé; or an appetizer flan and then a dessert custard.

3. I try to think about varying flavors (arugula, fennel, and radicchio salad with raisins) and colors (mixing different colored cherry or heirloom tomatoes or bell peppers).

4. I like to start with a first course, whether it's soup, a salad, a tart, pasta, a pizza, or even a couple of small plates. (I love firsts!)

5. I like to balance heavy and light dishes, richness, and intensity of flavor throughout the meal. If I start with a soup, I serve a substantial main, but if I start with a pizza, I'll serve a light main. If I've done pasta as a first, I won't have as much starch with my main course; if I've served a fairly substantial meal, I'll serve a lighter dessert like fresh fruit sorbet or ice cream and a cookie. If one course has been heavy on the butter and cream, the next will be light; if I have one highly flavored or spicy course, the next will be refined.

6. I always, always, *always* take seasonality into consideration. If it's summer, I'll celebrate it, whether with tomatoes, basil, or peaches. In winter, I like to use all those heartwarming, stick-to-your ribs comfort foods like butternut squash and Brussels sprouts, turnips, rutabagas, and parsnips.

7. I like to stay in the same country or region (like Asia or the Mediterranean) of dishes or ingredients. So I'll never serve a Japanese Miso Soup followed by Pasta with Italian Sausage or a Mexican stew followed by a Moroccan dessert. With ingredients, I might use the same family of ingredients— soy sauce, wasabi, and ginger, for example—throughout the meal, but I won't ever use soy sauce, wasabi, and ginger in one course and then balsamic vinegar and capers in the next.

    I do like American adaptations, like Fettuccine with Wild Mushrooms (page 71), but I don't like fusion.

8. I love diversity at the table, like skewers of salmon, pork, lamb, or chicken dipped in dry spice rub and served with a variety of sauces.

How to Survive Your Own Party

ONE WEEK TO SEVERAL DAYS BEFORE

* Plan your menu. Remember, no recipe is written in stone. If an ingredient isn't available or in season, try a substitute. Decide how you're going to serve the meal—individual plates or platters?

* Choreograph the evening. What time will people arrive; when will you serve the first course, etc. Remember to build some flexibility into this plan and to allow plenty of time for everything.

* Think about how you're going to style your table. Will you use flowers or candles (I use both and prefer low arrangements to encourage conversation at the table). What linens will you use—are they laundered? Is there anything you need to buy?

* Think about the music. Decide what you'll play. (I absolutely rely on my 5-CD disk changer; I set it up in advance with music for the whole evening!)

TWO DAYS BEFORE

* Clean your house. (Don't get too carried away with cleaning before the party; in my experience, cleaning up *after* the party requires the greater effort.)

ONE DAY BEFORE

* Shop for ingredients.
* Prep all the ingredients you possibly can.

DAY OF THE PARTY

* Morning: Set your table; complete any prep from day before; finish the dessert.
* Afternoon: Cook.
* Two-hours before guests arrive: Set out glasses and a large ice bucket and stock with sparkling water, still water, and champagne, white wine, or whatever

As a city forager, you've got to have a favorite wine shop, one where they sell good wine (of course!) and where they're generous and knowledgeable when it comes to giving advice. Look for a shop that has a good selection from different countries and regions and that stores wine on its side and in a cool, dark place.

Once you've found the right place, you need to find someone there who knows a lot about pairing food and wine. Even if you are already very informed, you can really benefit from the help of such a person. (I know food and wine pretty well and I *still* ask for ideas.) A good wine merchant will be familiar with the tastes of a particular wine and, if you can describe the food you're serving, will suggest several wines you might try. Be as specific as you can be about the dish you're serving and don't be afraid to ask about price.

Wine in Your Closet

If you live in the city, you may not have room for a large wine cellar and may find yourself eyeing that hallway linen closet (move out the sheets, move in a small wine collection). Or maybe you're just starting out and want to keep only a few bottles of wine in your house or apartment. I asked my good friend Tim McDonald, Director of Marketing Fine Wine Communications at Gallo Wines, for his advice on how to put together a small city wine cellar. Here's what he said.

1. Buy what you already know and like.
2. Find a wine writer that has a "palate" similar to your own. Read *The New York Times* on Wednesday; the *Wall Street Journal* on Friday; the *San Francisco Chronicle*

on Thursday; or the food and wine section of your local paper. Check out *The Wine Spectator* and *Wine and Spirits*. Buy some of the recommended wines and see if you agree with the reviewer.

3. Find a wine shop where you can talk with the buyer or another knowledgeable merchant.

4. Buy wines for drinking, not aging, when you're starting out.

Once you find what you like, how much should you get? Tim said that when you find a wine you like you should buy three to six bottles or a full case. Every six to nine months, break one open; you'll be able to "taste" the aging process as the wine develops. If you buy a couple of extra bottles every time you shop, your collection will develop pretty quickly.

Where should you store your wine collection? Wines like cool, dark, humid conditions, Tim said, but the single, most important thing is to find an area of your house or apartment where the temperature remains constant (wines are damaged by fluctuations in temperature).

The center of your house is a good bet, basements are terrific, or that closet—if it isn't on an outside wall—would work. Tim also said if you think you need additional temperature control, try wrapping your wine in mylar bubble wrap. Avoid areas near a water heater or another heat source, or where the wine will be subjected to vibrations (whether from a washing machine or heavy truck traffic). Also, don't store your wine near paint products or other chemicals, as it is possible that their smells can permeate the cork.

Store your wine on its side so that the wine is in contact with the cork to keep it moist and airtight. (If the cork shrinks, it can expose the contents of the bottle to oxygen and that could ruin your wine.)

How long should you store the wine? Tim said this really depends on the wine. A lot of wines made today are bred for early consumption. Well-balanced Cabernets, Syrahs, and Pinot Noirs, though, can be stored for six to ten years. However, all wines will benefit from a little rest after you've brought them home from the store. Good white wines need to rest for a few months, at least, or up to two to three years, depending upon the wine. A really good red like a Grand Cru Bordeaux, ought to rest from two to twenty years, again depending upon the particular wine and, of course, your patience.

Over Forty? (Starting a Forty-Something Wine Cellar)

Basically, the same recommendations apply whether you're stocking 40 or 400 bottles.

When I began building my collection, I tried to keep one thing in mind: balance. That is, a mixture of short-, medium- and long-term wines (I think of these as my Monday-through-Thursday, Weekend, and Special Occasion wines); and variety of grapes.

I tried to be global in scope, too, and collect wines from around the world. For example, reds from Piedmont and Tuscany in Italy; the Rhone, Burgundy, and Bordeaux in France; Rioja and Ribera del Duero from Spain; reds from South America; Shiraz from Australia; and, of course, reds from California. For whites, Sauvignon Blanc from New Zealand; Chardonnay and Riesling from Australia; a few Riesling and Gewürztraminer from Alsace, France; white burgundies from France; and a personal favorite, Sancerre, from the Loire Valley in France. There's always room for a few crisp whites from Italy. I include wines that will appeal to other people's tastes, not just my own. And always remember that there are no wrong choices and to have fun!

MONDAY-THROUGH-THURSDAY WINES (SHORT-TERM WINES)

These are the wines that I'll drink or serve during the week for casual meals or entertaining, my day-to-day wines, and the wines I'll use for cooking. There are many to choose from, but I look for wines in the $7 to $20 per bottle price range, including whites from California, New Zealand, Australia, France, and Italy; and reds from California's coastal regions, Australia, Italy, South America, Spain, and France.

WEEKEND WINES (MEDIUM-TERM WINES)

These are wines for more special occasions, like dinner parties and weekends. They have a three- to ten-year aging potential; are priced $12 to $30 per bottle; and there are lots of choices (and sometimes great bargains). I look for French red Burgundy and Bordeaux; Italian Chianti and Barbaresco; California Syrah and Zinfandel; Australian Shiraz; and whites from California (Sauvignon Blanc and Chardonnay), Alsace and the Loire, Tuscany, and New Zealand (Sauvignon Blanc).

SPECIAL OCCASION WINES (LONG-TERM WINES)

These are wines for important celebrations, dinners, parties, or gifts. They have a ten-year or longer aging potential, and prices start at $15, but can go very high. Most of these wines are reds. I look for Cabernets from known producers and Pinot Noir from California's Russian River and Carneros producers. I collect from Italy's Piedmont and Tuscany regions; France's Burgundy, Bordeaux, and northern Rhone; Spain's Rioja, Ribera del Duero, and Catalonia. I include in this category ports and Madeira from Portugal and Sauternes from France. It's also nice to have a few bottles of French champagne and California sparkling wines on hand.

WHAT I KEEP IN MY CELLAR

WHITES

Sauvignon Blancs, especially from New Zealand, California, and France
Dry Riesling from California, Alsace, Germany, or Australia
Pinot Gris from Oregon
Pinot Grigio from Italy
Chardonnay (I'm not a particularly oaky Chardonnay lover, but I know other people are, so I always have a few bottles on hand.)

ROSÉ

I especially like rosés from Spain or France, since they tend to be dry.

REDS

Pinot Noir from California's Russian River and Carneros producers and France
Zinfandels from California
Shiraz/Syrah from Australia and California
Cabernet Sauvignon from California and France
Merlot
Chianti from Tuscany

Is This Wine for Cooking or Drinking?

When I am asked how good a wine you need for cooking, I always say, "If you can't drink it, you can't cook with it." Does this mean that I'll use a bottle of 1966 French Bordeaux if a recipe calls for three cups of wine? No, I'll use a Monday-through-Thursday wine from my cellar.

There *are* times when the quality isn't that important. For example, when you make fish stock, an ordinary dry Sauvignon Blanc will be fine. On the other hand, when you make a dish like Risotto with Amarone or Risotto with Zinfandel, you're really going to taste the wine. So use something that you would enjoy drinking. In general, white wines for cooking should be light and acidic (like Sauvignon Blanc), and reds should be young and full-bodied (like Merlot, Cabernet Sauvignon, or Côtes du Rhône).

One happy, unintended benefit of using a drinkable wine to cook with is that you'll have perfectly paired your dish—if you serve the same wine you cooked with.

Top Ten Tips on Food and Wine Pairing

1. The weight and style of the food and the wine should match. Pair a grilled New York steak with a robust Cabernet—both are big in style and weight. Blue cheese and port or late-harvest wines—both have big, intense flavors. Sautéed sole in a light lemon butter would be really good alongside a delicate but rich Chardonnay.

2. Conventional wisdom used to hold that white wines went with white meat (chicken, pork, and fish) and red wines went with red meat (beef and lamb). But now I think more about matching the components of the dish than the meat itself. For example, if I'm serving a chicken breast with a romesco sauce or an olive relish, chances are that a lighter red wine will work.

3. Dishes from a certain region tend to go with wine from the same region. For example, in Provence, most of the white wines are lighter and go very well with clams, shrimp, and fresh fish out of the Mediterranean; in Tuscany the wine is predominately Sangiovese and it's higher acidity pairs quite well with tomato-based sauces and many meat dishes.

4. Less oaky wines are easier to pair with food; the oak flavor of a big Chardonnay, for example, can obliterate the fruit, which is why I like wines with just a kiss of oak.

5. Salt can bridge the flavors of sweet, sour, and bitter in food and make a dish more wine friendly.

6. Acidity is a friend. It brings out the fruit in the wine that pairs well with food.

7. Some people assume "food and wine pairing" implies only one match. This isn't correct; there are many possible matches. Try different combinations and discover what you like.

8. Sparkling wine is really food-friendly. So if all else fails, choose sparkling wine or champagne.

9. Don't be afraid to ask the advice of others, including the chef or server in a restaurant.

10. Drink what you like to drink with what you like to eat. It's your palate and that means you tend to crave certain flavors which, in turn, are likely to go together.

WINES BY WEIGHT

Light white: Sauvignon Blanc, Riesling, Pinot Gris, Pinot Grigio, Gewürztraminer

Medium-bodied white: Chardonnay

Light-bodied red: Beaujolais, Chianti, Bandolino

Medium-bodied red: Pinot Noir, Merlot, Zinfandel, Côtes du Rhône, Chianti Classico, and some Cabernet Sauvignon

Hearty red: Cabernet Sauvignon, Barolo, Barbaresco, and some Zinfandel, Merlot, French Bordeaux, and Shiraz

---

TOP TEN CLASSIC PAIRINGS

1. Sauvignon Blanc with goat cheese.
2. Cabernets and Bordeaux with beef.
3. Fruitier wines like Riesling or Gewürztraminer with Asian dishes.
4. Pinot Noirs with turkey, chicken, duck, pheasant, and just about everything.
5. Pinot Noir, Red Burgundy, or Chardonnay with grilled salmon and other fatty fish.
6. Pinot Gris or Pinot Grigio with lighter dishes like shrimp, scallops, and salads.
7. Chardonnay with roast chicken or sautéed fish.
8. Zinfandel with grilled or barbecued dishes.
9. Sparkling wine with smoked salmon-and-caviar pizza.
10. Champagne with salty foods.

The Neighborhoods

From a distance, say, from a travel book, a map, or from the air, our cities can take on the appearance of a single, unified place with only their outer boundaries to define them. But move in closer, live there or visit for more than a few days, and the constituent parts begin to reveal themselves: the 200-year-old neighborhood of Italians or Chinese; the new neighborhood of immigrant Hispanics or thirty-something-year-olds re-creating a neighborhood in their own image.

All great cities have their share of business and culture districts. But in some ways, it's the residential neighborhoods that give the city its energy and richness. They say Chicago is a city of neighborhoods. New York's and Los Angeles's neighborhoods are famous to all of us, even if we've never been to them: Brooklyn, Soho, Beverly Hills, Watts. In San Francisco, the neighborhoods are named after streets or nature, but also after the dominant ethnic population living there.

And isn't that fitting? After all, the neighborhoods are where we live, where we raise our kids, have Sunday dinner with our families, visit with our friends. We pick them because our parents or grandparents, a friend, or other people from the country we've just left live there. Wherever we come from, we bring our culture and our cooking with us. We open restaurants and markets, and fill them with our food. We create these diverse neighborhoods, with one country's food integrating with another or just being itself.

When I walk in my neighborhood each morning, I can pass through three distinct food neighborhoods. I can go south to Japantown for Asian ingredients; north to the Fillmore for the bakeries, cheese, and wine shops; west to the best butcher. I can hop on my motor scooter and be in the Mission in a few minutes where I can get the most incredible burritos or stop at my favorite Mexican market there and buy all of the ingredients I need—fresh limes, chiles, and warm corn tortillas—to make my own at home. Or I can go out to the Haight, with its incredibly complex social history (from riches to rags to riches again) and everything from vintage clothing shops to those selling the latest street fashions, and just sit and watch the scene while eating falafel, the perfect street food.

Our city neighborhoods are there for the exploring; rich with the tastes and flavors of our own and the world's cultures. We've got to get out there; try new dishes; go to the old, traditional establishments that have marked our cities' culinary maps for generations and to the newest; to look for long lines at small places; and then to come home and cook and create.

Rice Paper Shrimp Rolls

Vietnamese rice paper salad rolls can be filled with all kinds of goodies from alfalfa sprouts, cellophane noodles, shredded lettuce, and Thai basil to slivered chicken, but I particularly like this combination. I order them every time I eat in the Vietnamese restaurant in my neighborhood. The only problem is that one order is never enough! There's something about sweet, savory, hot, and sour all rolled into one little bite; you can't eat just one.

ROLLS

$^3/_4$ pound large shrimp

$^1/_2$ cup coarsely grated carrots

$^1/_4$ cup finely chopped scallions

$^3/_4$ cup napa or Savoy cabbage, thinly sliced

1 tablespoon rice vinegar

Salt

9 rice paper rounds (8-inch diameter)

4 butter lettuce leaves, ribs removed

$^1/_2$ cup fresh mint leaves

$^3/_4$ cup cilantro leaves

Cilantro sprigs as a garnish

DIPPING SAUCE

2 teaspoons vegetable oil

2 cloves garlic, minced

$^1/_4$ teaspoon crushed red pepper

$^2/_3$ cup water

2 tablespoons creamy peanut butter

2 tablespoons hoisin sauce

1 tablespoon tomato paste

$^1/_4$ teaspoon sugar

1 teaspoon hot chili sauce

2 tablespoons raw, unsalted peanuts, toasted

Make the rolls: Shell the shrimp and devein. Bring one cup of water to a boil in a large skillet over high heat. Add the shrimp and cook just until they start to turn pink, about 1 minute. Turn off the heat and let the shrimp cool in the water for 20 minutes. Halve each shrimp lengthwise.

In a bowl, toss together the carrots, scallions, cabbage and the vinegar. Season with salt.

Place a double thickness of paper towel on a work surface. Fill a large shallow baking pan with warm water. Soak 1 rice paper round at a time (make sure there are no holes) in the water until pliable, 30 to 60 seconds. Transfer to the paper towels. Repeat with the remaining rice paper rounds, placing them on the paper towels in a single layer. Cover with slightly dampened paper towels.

Place 1 piece of softened rice paper on the work surface. Arrange ½ piece lettuce on the bottom half of the rice paper, folding and tearing the lettuce leaf to fit and leaving a 1-inch border along the edge. Divide the shrimp into 8 portions and place one-eighth on the lettuce. Top with one-eighth of the vegetable mixture. Top with one-eighth of the mint and cilantro leaves. Roll the filling tightly inside the rice paper, folding in the two sides of the rice paper to make a compact roll. Repeat with the remaining rice paper rounds and filling ingredients to make a total of 8 rolls.

Make the dipping sauce: In a small saucepan, warm the oil over medium heat. Add the garlic and crushed red pepper and cook, stirring, until the garlic is light golden. Whisk in the water, peanut butter, hoisin sauce, tomato paste, water and sugar, and bring to a boil. Simmer the sauce, whisking, until thickened, 30 to 60 seconds. Place in a small bowl and spoon the chili sauce into the center. Garnish with toasted peanuts. The sauce can be made 3 days in advance and refrigerated until ready to use.

To serve, cut the rolls in half on the sharp diagonal. Place on a platter and serve with the sauce on the side.

SERVES 6

WINE SUGGESTION: Grüner Vetliner or Viognier

Potato Rosemary Flatbread

San Francisco boasts some of the best breads in the world, with sourdough being the most famous. We have a slew of fantastic bakeries including Acme, Bay Bread, and Tartine, to name just a few. (There's even an incredible French bakery, La Boulangerie, in my neighborhood.) At the drop of a hat, I can buy every shape, texture, and flavor of bread I desire. That is all well and good and I take advantage of it every chance I get. But when I want the smell of fresh bread in my kitchen, this delicious flatbread fits the bill.

6 tablespoons extra-virgin olive oil

4 sprigs fresh rosemary plus 1 tablespoon whole rosemary leaves

2 cups water

Kosher salt

2 small waxy brown potatoes, thinly sliced (about 6 ounces)

2¹/₂ teaspoons active dry yeast

2¹/₂ cup cups unbleached bread flour

In a small saucepan, warm the olive oil and rosemary sprigs. Remove from the heat and set aside for 1 hour. Discard the rosemary sprigs.

Meanwhile, put the water in a saucepan, salt it, and bring to a boil. Add the potatoes and cook until tender, 3 to 5 minutes. Drain, reserving 1 cup of the potato water; discard the remaining water. Let the potatoes cool separately.

Place the potato water in a saucepan and heat to 110°F. In a large bowl, mix the yeast and ¹/₂ cup warm potato water. Stir in ¹/₂ cup of the flour. Let stand for 1 hour until it bubbles and rises. Add the remaining 2 cups flour, 4 tablespoons of the infused rosemary oil, remaining ¹/₂ cup potato water, and 1 teaspoon salt. Mix dough thoroughly. Knead on a floured board until soft yet still moist, 7 to 8 minutes. Place the dough in an oiled bowl, turning once. Cover bowl with plastic wrap and place in a warm spot (about 75°F). Let rise for 1 to 2 hours until doubled in volume.

Thirty minutes before baking, preheat the oven to 500°F. Place a pizza stone on the bottom rack of the oven. Form the dough into a round ball. Let rest for 5 minutes. On a floured surface, roll out the dough to form a 9 x 12-inch oval, ½ inch thick. Transfer to a well-floured pizza peel. Drizzle the remaining 2 tablespoons infused rosemary on top. Sprinkle the rosemary leaves on top. Place the potatoes on the dough and press them in slightly. Sprinkle with salt. Let rest for 10 minutes. Transfer the flatbread directly onto the pizza stone and bake until golden brown and crispy, 12 to 15 minutes.

MAKES 1 FLATBREAD; SERVES 6

WINE SUGGESTION: Chardonnay or Merlot

> *"You wouldn't think such a place as San Francisco could exist. The wonderful sunlight there, the hills, the great bridges, the Pacific at your shoes. Beautiful Chinatown. Every race in the world. The sardine fleets sailing out. The little cable cars whizzing down the city hills…And all the people are open and friendly."*
>
> DYLAN THOMAS

Phyllo Pizza with Feta and Tomatoes

I have my favorite places in the city to get pizza; one is right in my neighborhood! I also love to make pizza at home and encourage you to try it if you haven't. But if making pizza dough still seems a little intimidating to you, instead of making yeast dough, make the pizza crust with sheets of phyllo, the paper-thin dough used in many Middle Eastern dishes and available in most grocery stores. If you can, buy the phyllo fresh rather than frozen (if you can only get frozen phyllo, defrost it in the package). When you are ready to make the phyllo pizza, remove the phyllo from the wrapper and cover it with a barely dampened kitchen towel (keep this on the whole time). Don't worry if some of the sheets are torn. . . . Who's going to see it when it's between all those layers?

> 10 sheets phyllo dough
>
> 3 tablespoons butter
>
> 3 tablespoons extra-virgin olive oil
>
> 3/4 cup coarsely grated mozzarella cheese (about 3 ounces)
>
> 3/4 cup finely crumbled feta cheese (about 3 ounces)
>
> 1/2 cup grated Kefalotyri or Parmigiano-Reggiano cheese
>
> 1 teaspoon dried oregano
>
> Salt
>
> 4 scallions, white and green parts, thinly sliced
>
> 1 pint (2 cups) yellow, red, and orange cherry tomatoes, halved

Cut the stack of phyllo sheets in half widthwise to make 2 stacks approximately 9 inches by 12 inches. Cover the stacks with a barely dampened towel. Melt the butter in a small saucepan over medium-low heat. Add the oil and stir together. In a bowl, combine the mozzarella, feta, Kefalotyri, oregano, and salt to taste.

Preheat the oven to 400°F. Lightly oil a large baking sheet with the butter-oil mixture. Place one piece of phyllo in the center of the baking sheet. Using a pastry brush, lightly brush the phyllo with the butter-oil mixture. Place another layer of

phyllo directly on top. Brush lightly with the butter-oil mixture. Repeat with one more layer. You now have three layers of phyllo on the pan. Sprinkle with a scant 2 tablespoons of the combined cheeses. Continue with three more layers of phyllo, brushing lightly with butter-oil between each layer. Sprinkle with another scant 2 tablespoons of the combined cheeses. Continue until you have used all of the phyllo. If the butter-oil mixture gets cold in the meantime, warm it on the stove.

Brush the top layer with the butter-oil mixture. Sprinkle with half of the remaining cheese. Sprinkle the scallions and then the tomatoes evenly over the top of the pizza, leaving a 1-inch border around the edge. Season the tomatoes with salt and sprinkle the remaining cheese on top. Trim the edges if desired.

Bake on the top shelf of the oven until the cheese is melted and the phyllo is golden and crisp on the edges, 20 to 30 minutes.

SERVES 6

WINE SUGGESTION: Pinot Gris, Pinot Grigio, Sangiovese, or Chianti

---

"For years, we've been walking to Chinatown for lunch. The custom began as a way of showing out-of-town visitors some of lower Manhattan. Starting out in the Village, we'd walk through the Italian South Village, through Soho…through Little Italy, and finally to Chinatown, where we'd have dim sum lunch."

CALVIN TRILLIN

Croutons with Tapenade, Orange, and Fennel

Tapenade—a paste made from olives, capers, and anchovies—is a Provençal staple in the south of France. Delicious served as a condiment with grilled tuna or a roasted lamb sandwich, it's also great as a dip for a warm baguette or fresh seasonal vegetables. I have taken a little spin from the traditional paste to add orange and fennel, two ingredients that marry well with olives.

Tightly covered, tapenade may be kept in the refrigerator for up to a week.

1 cup pitted Niçoise or Kalamata olives

2 cloves garlic, minced

1 tablespoon capers, chopped

2 anchovy fillets, soaked in cold water for 5 minutes, patted dry, and mashed

2 tablespoons extra-virgin olive oil

1½ tablespoons orange juice

2 teaspoons orange zest

1 teaspoon fennel seeds, coarsely ground

Freshly ground black pepper

12 slices good-quality firm country-style bread, toasted and cut into 2-inch pieces

Orange wedges as a garnish

Flat-leaf parsley sprigs as a garnish

In a food processor, pulse three-quarters of the olives, the garlic, capers, anchovies, olive oil, orange juice, orange zest, and fennel seeds until almost smooth. Add the rest of the olives and pulse a few more times to make a coarse-textured paste. Season with pepper.

Toast the bread either on an outdoor grill, under a broiler, or in a toaster. To serve, spread the tapenade onto the croutons and place on a platter. Garnish with orange wedges and parsley sprigs and serve immediately.

MAKES ABOUT 1¼ CUPS TAPENADE; SERVES 6

WINE SUGGESTION: Champagne, Sauvignon Blanc, or Pinot Noir

Crostini with Dried Plum Paste and Goat Cheese

Who would have ever thought that in our lifetime the name for prunes would be changed to "dried plums"? No matter what you call them, they are good for you: high in fiber and potassium and low in fat. I have always loved them any old way...even straight out of the bag as a quick snack. But pair them with goat cheese on a toasted crostini and you have a sweet and tart treat. Don't forget a glass of Sauvignon Blanc—it pairs perfectly!

> 1 cup pitted dried plums or prunes (6 ounces)
> 1/2 cup orange juice
> 1/2 cup water
> 2 teaspoons grated orange zest
> Pinch of salt
> 18 baguette slices, sliced on a sharp diagonal
> 5 ounces fresh goat cheese, at room temperature
> 1 scallion, minced

Place the dried plums, orange juice, water, orange zest, and salt in a saucepan. Simmer over low heat until the dried plums are soft and 2 tablespoons of the liquid remains, 15 to 20 minutes. Let the mixture cool and then puree in a blender or food processor to make a paste. Reserve.

Toast the baguette slices. Spread the dried plum paste evenly on top of the crostini.

Place the goat cheese in a bowl and mash. Spread about 1/2 tablespoon goat cheese over the dried plum paste. Sprinkle the scallions on top and serve.

SERVES 6

WINE SUGGESTION: Sauvignon Blanc, dry Riesling, or a light Shiraz

Smoked Eggplant with Pita Chips

The distinctive smoky flavor of this puree is achieved by roasting the eggplant over an open flame. If you don't have a gas stove, you can achieve the same effect on an outdoor grill. Alternatively, you can use the broiler on your oven: cut the eggplant in half and place it on an oiled baking sheet, cut side up, under the broiler until the skin is wrinkled and black. It won't taste quite as smoky; but on the other hand, it's a convenient and easy alternative. You can make this puree up to two days in advance and store it in the refrigerator until ready to use. Just bring it to room temperature before serving.

2 large eggplants

3 pita bread pockets (8-inch diameter)

1/4 cup extra-virgin olive oil

Salt

Freshly ground black pepper

4 cloves garlic, minced

1/2 teaspoon sweet paprika

1/4 teaspoon ground cumin

Pinch of crushed red pepper

1 tablespoon lemon juice

Black olives as a garnish (Kalamata or Niçoise)

Lemon wedges as a garnish

1 teaspoon chopped fresh flat-leaf parsley as a garnish

Preheat the oven to 375°F. Place the eggplant directly on the high flame of a gas stove, turning constantly until the skin is black and wrinkled, 7 to 10 minutes. Place the eggplant on a baking sheet and bake the eggplant in the oven until very soft, 15 to 20 minutes.

In the meantime, split each pita pocket into 2 separate rounds. Cut each round into 8 wedges. Place the pita wedges on a baking sheet. Drizzle with 3 tablespoons of the olive oil, sprinkle with salt and pepper, and toss together. Bake in the oven, tossing occasionally, until crisp, 10 to 12 minutes. Remove from the oven and let cool on the baking sheet.

When the eggplant are soft and cooked through, remove from the oven and let cool 5 minutes. Cut the eggplant in half, scoop out the pulp, and chop coarsely.

Discard the skin. Sprinkle with salt and let drain in a paper towel–lined colander for 10 minutes. With the back of a spoon, press the eggplant to extract any additional liquid; discard.

In a large bowl, mash the eggplant. Add the garlic, paprika, cumin, crushed red pepper, and 1 tablespoon remaining olive oil and mix well. Season with salt, pepper, and the lemon juice.

Place the puree on a plate and garnish with black olives, lemon wedges, and parsley. Serve with the crispy pita chips.

SERVES 6

WINE SUGGESTION: Arneis, Vernacia, Pinot Noir, or Barbera

"A great city is that which has the greatest men and women."

WALT WHITMAN

Pita Chips with Cucumbers, Feta, Dill, and Mint

This is one of my favorite dishes when I am in a rush. And if I'm *really* pressed for time, I'll serve it with fresh pita bread cut into wedges rather than the chips.

PITA CHIPS

3 pita bread pockets (8-inch diameter)

3 tablespoons extra-virgin olive oil

Salt and freshly ground black pepper

TOPPING

8 ounces feta cheese

1 medium English cucumber, peeled, seeded, and cut into ¼-inch dice

1 small red onion, cut into ¼-inch dice

3 tablespoons chopped fresh mint

3 tablespoons chopped fresh dill

2½ tablespoons fresh lemon juice

1 tablespoon extra-virgin olive oil

Sprigs of mint as a garnish

3 lemon wedges as a garnish

Make the pita chips: Preheat the oven to 375°F. Split each pita pocket into 2 separate rounds. Cut each round into 8 wedges. Place the pita wedges on a baking sheet. Drizzle with the olive oil, sprinkle with salt and pepper, and toss. Bake, tossing occasionally, until crisp, 10 to 12 minutes. Remove from the oven and let cool on the baking sheet.

Make the topping: Crumble the feta into a bowl and stir together with the cucumber, onion, mint, dill, lemon juice, and olive oil.

Place the topping in a small bowl and garnish with mint and lemon wedges. Place the bowl in the center of a larger serving platter. Surround with the pita chips and serve.

SERVES 6

WINE SUGGESTION: Sauvignon Blanc

Bagna Cauda, a Warm Italian Bath

When you think bagna cauda, think fondue with a twist. This Italian dish is basically tons of garlic and anchovies bathed in hot olive oil and butter. For a real treat, use an authentic bagna cauda pot, an earthenware bowl warmed underneath by a candle. Dip any seasonal vegetables or breadsticks into the "bath," but go easy: it's deceptively rich.

BAGNA CAUDA
8 whole salted anchovies or 16
   oil-cured anchovy fillets
6 tablespoons unsalted butter
12 cloves garlic, minced
1½ cups extra-virgin olive oil

ACCOMPANIMENTS
breadsticks
sliced fresh fennel

sliced carrots
scallions
green onions
red bell pepper strips
cooked potatoes
raw cauliflower florets
sliced cardoons
cucumbers
cherry tomatoes

Soak the whole anchovies in cold water for 5 minutes. Discard the water. Fillet the anchovies and soak them again in another bowl of cold water for 10 minutes. Pat the anchovies dry and mash into a paste.

Melt the butter over low heat in a heavy saucepan. Add the garlic and cook for 10 minutes over very low heat. Do not let the garlic brown; it should be very lightly golden. Add the anchovies and olive oil and cook gently, stirring occasionally, for 30 minutes.

Place the bagna cauda in the center of the table and pass the accompaniments alongside.

SERVES 6

WINE SUGGESTION: Barbera

Prosciutto, Parmigiano, and Pepper Breadsticks

In America, we call them breadsticks; in Italy, they call them *grissini*. Whatever you call them, most Americans think of breadsticks as tasteless, pencil-like sticks of toast wrapped in waxy envelopes and served at bad Italian restaurants. But when homemade *grissini* are flavored with crispy prosciutto, Parmigiano, and a good dose of coarsely cracked black and red pepper and served hot from the oven, there're utterly delicious. Serve with drinks or as an accompaniment to soups, salads, or, of course, a platter of antipasti. Or try my personal favorite: Wrap a thin strip of prosciutto around the top half and serve.

> 4 thin slices prosciutto (about 2 ounces)
> 1 1/2 cups warm water (about 110°F)
> 2 teaspoons active dry yeast
> 4 cups bread flour
> 2 tablespoons extra-virgin olive oil
> 1 tablespoon coarsely ground black pepper
> 1 3/4 teaspoons salt
> Pinch of cayenne pepper
> 1 cup finely grated Parmigiano-Reggiano cheese
> 1/4 cup semolina

Preheat the oven to 400°F. Place the prosciutto in a single layer on a baking sheet and bake until very crispy, dry, and light golden brown, 7 to 8 minutes. Cool the prosciutto and crumble into tiny pieces.

In a bowl, combine 1/2 cup warm water and the yeast. Stir in 1/2 cup flour. Let stand until the mixture bubbles and rises slightly, 30 minutes. Add the remaining 3 1/2 cups flour and 1 cup warm water, and the prosciutto, olive oil, black pepper, salt, and cayenne. Stir together to form a ball. Knead on a lightly floured surface, kneading in the Parmigiano gradually, until smooth and elastic, 7 to 10 minutes. Alternatively this can be made in an electric mixer on low speed using the dough hook, kneading for 5 minutes.

Using your hands, shape the dough into an 5 x 15-inch rectangle. Brush with oil, cover loosely with plastic wrap, and let rise in a warm spot (about 75°F) until doubled in volume, 1 to 1^1/$_4$ hours.

Thirty minutes before baking, preheat the oven to 450°F.

Cut the dough lengthwise into 5 equal 1-inch strips. Cut the dough crosswise into 5 sections. This will make 25 pieces. Pick up each piece of dough and roll and stretch to fit the width of a baking sheet, dusting with semolina if necessary. Place in a single layer 1 inch apart on an oiled baking sheet that has been dusted with semolina. Bake in the middle of the oven until light golden, 10 to 12 minutes. Turn the breadsticks and continue to bake until golden and crispy, 2 to 3 minutes longer. Remove from the oven and let cool on a cooling rack.

MAKES 25 BREADSTICKS

WINE SUGGESTION: Merlot, Zinfandel, or champagne

Fiery Peppered Feta with Pita

My first trip to Turkey was a real eye-opener. I never realized how wonderful, fresh, and flavorful Turkish food was until I visited there. I was in the little village of Go,reme and as soon as someone found out what I did for a living, I had a new friend: Fatima, the owner of the inn where I was staying. She got the village women together to make a meze lunch (meze are the Turkish equivalent of tapas). We gathered around a table for the whole afternoon and ate plate after plate of meze. This dish happened to be one of my absolute favorites. It's really simple, and combined with the fact that it can be made a day in advance, ideal for entertaining. (If you make it ahead, refrigerate it and then bring it to room temperature before serving.)

10 ounces feta cheese

1 cup yogurt, drained in a paper-towel-lined sieve for 4 hours

Salt

2 cloves garlic, minced

1 1/2 tablespoons extra-virgin olive oil

1 1/2 teaspoons sweet paprika, plus more for sprinkling

1/4 teaspoon cayenne pepper

Freshly ground black pepper

Black olives as a garnish (such as Kalamata)

3 fresh pita breads (8-inch diameter), each cut into 8 to 12 wedges

Preheat the oven to 400°F.

Place the feta, yogurt, and 1/4 teaspoon salt in a bowl and mash with a fork to make a smooth paste. Alternatively this can be pureed in a food processor. Add the garlic, 1 tablespoon of the olive oil, paprika, and cayenne. Season with salt and black pepper and mix well.

Wrap the pita tightly in foil and place in the oven until warm, about 10 minutes.

Spread the feta puree on a serving plate. Drizzle with the remaining ½ table-spoon olive oil, sprinkle with paprika, and garnish with olives. Serve with the warm pita.

SERVES 6

WINE SUGGESTION: Riesling, Gewürztraminer, Shiraz, or Syrah

STREET FOOD

Pita Chips with Cucumbers, Feta, Dill, and Mint (page 57)
Fiery Peppered Feta with Pita (page 62)
Falafel with Tahini and Herb Salad (page 64)
Roasted Pepper Salad with Eggplant Croutons (page 101)

Falafel with Tahini and Herb Salad

I've had a long love affair with Mediterranean food, especially food from the Middle East. I was introduced to this kind of food by my Lebanese friend, Pamela, when we went to art school together. Later, I moved to Boston and discovered a restaurant in my neighborhood called "The Middle East." Whenever I needed something redolent with garlic and lemon, I would stop and get a falafel sandwich.

Falafel is street food at its best. Serve them with this herb salad or, more traditionally, tuck the falafel into pockets of warm pita bread and smother with tahini.

FALAFEL

9 ounces dry chickpeas (1½ cups)

2 tablespoons medium fine bulgur or cracked wheat

¼ cup boiling water

1 medium onion, finely chopped

½ cup chopped fresh cilantro leaves

⅓ cup chopped fresh flat-leaf parsley leaves

10 cloves garlic, minced

2 tablespoons ground cumin

1 tablespoon ground coriander

1 teaspoon turmeric

1 teaspoon baking soda

¼ to ½ teaspoon cayenne pepper, depending upon your taste

Salt and freshly ground black pepper

Vegetable oil for deep frying

SALAD

2 tablespoons extra-virgin olive oil

1 tablespoon lemon juice

2 cups mixed baby salad greens

1 cup fresh cilantro leaves

1 cup fresh flat-leaf parsley leaves

20 fresh mint leaves

2 cups tahini sauce (recipe follows)

Make the falafel: Pick over chickpeas and discard any stones. Cover beans with water and soak overnight.

Place bulgur in a bowl and cover with the boiling water. Stir well and let stand for 30 minutes.

After the chickpeas have soaked, place them in a food processor with the onion, and process until they form a crumbly paste. Add the bulgur, cilantro, parsley, garlic, cumin, coriander, turmeric, baking soda, and cayenne. Season to taste with salt and black pepper and pulse a few times to mix well. Remove from the processor, place in a bowl, and set aside for 30 minutes.

Shape the falafel into walnut-size balls and flatten slightly. Place on a baking sheet and let rest for 30 minutes. These can be prepared up to this point 24 hours in advance.

In a large, deep skillet, heat 1 inch of oil to 375°F. Shallow-fry the falafel, a few at a time, until they are golden on both sides, 2 to 3 minutes. The falafel can be kept warm in a 400°F oven until ready to serve for up to 10 minutes.

Make the salad: In a bowl, whisk together the olive oil and lemon juice. Season with salt and black pepper. Toss the greens, cilantro, parsley, and mint with the dressing. Place the salad on a platter and top with the hot falafel. Serve immediately with a bowl of tahini alongside.

MAKES 30 FALAFEL; SERVES 6

WINE SUGGESTION: Sauvignon Blanc

Tahini

⅓ cup sesame paste or tahini

¼ cup lemon juice

¼ cup water

3 cloves garlic, mashed to a paste

1 teaspoon ground cumin

Salt

In a food processor or blender, combine all of the ingredients except the salt. Pulse a few times until smooth. Season with salt. Thin with 2 to 3 tablespoons additional water to make a barely fluid paste.

MAKES 1 CUP

Chicken Lettuce Wraps

This is one of those dishes that I *have* to order every single time I go to Chinatown and see them on the menu. I love the crunch of the lettuce, the saltiness of the soy sauce, and the sweetness of the oyster sauce. You can substitute turkey, pork, or squab with equally delicious results.

2 tablespoons peanut oil

1 pound ground dark meat chicken

8 scallions, white and green parts, minced

2 teaspoons cornstarch

$^2/_3$ cup water chestnuts, chopped

3 tablespoons soy sauce

1 tablespoon grated fresh ginger

1 tablespoon oyster sauce

1 large head butter lettuce, leaves separated

Warm the oil in a skillet or wok over medium-high heat. Add the chicken, scallions, and cornstarch and cook, stirring constantly, until the chicken is cooked and broken into pieces, 3 to 4 minutes. Add the water chestnuts, soy sauce, ginger, and oyster sauce and cook for 1 minute. Remove from the heat.

To serve, take 1 lettuce leaf at a time and spoon a heaping tablespoon of the chicken mixture into the center. Wrap the lettuce around the filling. Serve.

SERVES 6

WINE SUGGESTION: Gewürztraminer, Pinot Gris, or Pinot Grigio

Dried Plums Stuffed with Gorgonzola and Walnuts

I love all three of these ingredients, so when I put them together I was in heaven. Simple to make, these little nuggets of sweetness make a great cold-weather first to serve before the meal with drinks.

> $1/4$ cup walnuts (about 1 ounce)
> 2 ounces Gorgonzola cheese, at room temperature
> 32 dried plums, pitted

Preheat the oven to 375°F. Place the walnuts on a baking sheet and toast until light golden, 5 to 7 minutes. Let cool, then chop.

With a small knife, make a slit on the side of each dried plum.

In a bowl, mash the walnuts and Gorgonzola together. Spoon into a pastry bag fitted with a $1/2$-inch tip. Pipe a small marble-size piece of the mixture into each dried plum, distributing evenly. Serve.

SERVES 8

WINE SUGGESTION: Dry sherry like fino, manzanilla, or amontillado

Parmesan Flan

The first time I made this recipe was with my students in the Piedmont area of Italy. I remember the day well—we were eating al fresco overlooking the vines of the Piedmont on one of the most beautiful days. The sky was the brightest blue and there wasn't a cloud in it. As we toasted to a really fun and productive cooking class, I thought, I may have the best job in the world. Then I tasted the flan and was convinced! These flans are really easy to make and are perfect served as a first course or a light main course for lunch.

3 tablespoons butter

3 tablespoons flour

1 cup milk

3 eggs

2 egg yolks

2 cups finely grated Parmigiano-Reggiano cheese (about 8 ounces)

Salt and freshly ground black pepper

Boiling water for the baking dish

2 tablespoons extra-virgin olive oil

2½ cups peeled, seeded, and chopped tomatoes (fresh or canned)

20 basil leaves

Preheat the oven to 375°F. Generously butter six 5-ounce ramekins.

Melt the butter in a medium saucepan over medium heat. Add the flour and whisk for 3 minutes. Slowly add the milk, whisking constantly, and cook, stirring until it thickens, about 3 minutes. Transfer the mixture to a bowl and add the eggs, Whisk well. Add the cheese, season with salt and pepper, and stir until well mixed.

Pour the mixture into the prepared ramekins. Place in a baking dish. Pour in enough boiling water to come 1 inch up the sides of the ramekins. Bake until the flans are puffed and firm to the touch, 30 minutes.

Meanwhile, warm the olive oil in a large skillet over medium-high heat. Add the tomatoes and heat until hot, 1 to 2 minutes. Season with salt and pepper.

When the flans are done, remove them from the water bath. Run a knife around the edge and remove the flans from the ramekins.

To serve, place one flan in the center of each plate. Spoon the tomato sauce onto the top and around the sides of the flans. Cut the basil into thin strips and garnish the flans.

SERVES 6

WINE SUGGESTION: Barbera or Dolcetto

DINNER AT THE VILLA

Parmesan Flan (page 69)

Truffle-Scented Roasted Cornish Hens with Prosciutto and Wild
Mushrooms (page 180)

Pear Granita (page 307)

Fettuccine with Wild Mushrooms

This is an amazing dish, perfect for those months from mid-fall through winter when the rainy weather brings wild mushrooms to life in the forests. It's a dish to serve when you want something comforting but also decadent, creamy, and just incredibly delicious. It is very easy to make, yet it has such deep and rich flavor from the reduction of the dried porcini soaking liquid that is added to the sauce. (My friend says this is the best pasta dish she has had outside Italy.)

I use cultivated mushrooms, but if you've just foraged for wild mushrooms and have a lot that you know are absolutely safe, by all means substitute them for the cultivated ones. Also, even though this fettuccine recipe produces the most beautiful, satiny pasta, you can substitute a good-quality dried pasta with wonderful results.

I like to serve this as a first course, followed by Pan-Seared Chicken Breasts with Mustard, Rosemary, and Capers (page 173) and a green salad.

1 ounce dried porcini mushrooms

1½ cups boiling water

1 cup heavy cream

3 cups homemade chicken stock or canned reduced-sodium broth

2 tablespoons unsalted butter

1½ pounds button or cultivated mushrooms, thinly sliced

Salt and freshly ground black pepper

1 pound fresh homemade fettuccine (recipe follows)

1 cup grated Parmigiano-Reggiano cheese

Place the dried porcini mushrooms in a heatproof bowl. Pour the boiling water over the mushrooms and set them aside until the water is cool, about 30 minutes.

Meanwhile, place the heavy cream in a saucepan and simmer until reduced by half. Reserve. Place the chicken stock in another saucepan and simmer until reduced to ½ cup. Reserve.

When the mushrooms are cool, remove with a slotted spoon and squeeze over the bowl. Reserve. Strain the soaking liquid in a sieve lined with a coffee filter or cheesecloth. Place the liquid in a saucepan and simmer until reduced to ¼ cup. Reserve.

In a large skillet, melt the butter over medium-high heat. Add the sliced fresh mushrooms and cook, stirring occasionally, until the mushrooms give off liquid and the liquid evaporates, 8 to 12 minutes. Add the porcini mushrooms and stir together. Add the reduced cream, chicken stock, and mushroom soaking liquid. Season with salt and pepper. Stir until mixed.

Bring a large pot of salted water to a boil. Add the pasta and cook until al dente, 3 to 4 minutes. In the meantime, warm the mushroom sauce over medium-high heat. Drain the pasta and add the mushroom sauce and half of the Parmigiano-Reggiano. Toss together and serve immediately, garnished with the remaining Parmigiano-Reggiano.

SERVES 6

WINE SUGGESTION: Chardonnay

Fresh Fettuccine

1½ cups all-purpose flour, plus more for kneading

½ cup very finely ground semolina

¼ teaspoon salt

2 whole eggs

1 tablespoon water

In a food processor, pulse together the flour, semolina, and salt many times. Add the eggs and water and process until the dough forms a soft ball but is not sticky. If necessary, add more flour a tablespoon at a time until it isn't sticky. Transfer the dough to a very lightly floured work surface and knead until soft and smooth, 2 to 3 minutes. Wrap the dough in plastic wrap and let rest for at least 30 minutes.

Divide the dough into 3 pieces. With a pasta machine, roll out 1 piece of pasta to a ⅛-inch thickness, or so you can almost see your hand through it. Roll the sheet through the fettuccine cutter. Cut the fettuccine into 10- to 12-inch strands and toss on your work surface with flour. Place on a baking sheet lined with a kitchen towel that has been heavily floured. Set aside and roll out the remaining 2 pieces of pasta.

MAKES APPROXIMATELY 1 POUND

> *"I don't know of any other city where you can walk through so many culturally diverse neighborhoods, and you're never out of sight of the wild hills. Nature is very close [in San Francisco]."*
>
> GARY SNYDER

Baked Eggs with Summer Vegetables

I've never been a big breakfast person. Maybe it's because the food is so often sweet and I tend to prefer savory before sweet. Or maybe it's because my whole life is about eating and dieting, and it seems that if I start eating too much too early, I'm lost in guilt for the whole day. But I do love these Spanish-inspired baked eggs. You can use any kind of vegetable, depending upon what's in season. And the best part is that you can get the whole dish assembled a day in advance and just bake it at the last minute. Served with Jalapeño-Jack Scones with Chive Butter (page 77) and a Bellini (page 315) or mimosa, *now* we're talking breakfast!

2 tablespoons extra-virgin olive oil

1 large onion, chopped

3 cloves garlic, minced

2¼ cups peeled, seeded, chopped, and drained tomatoes (canned or fresh)

1 tablespoon balsamic vinegar

1½ teaspoons sweet paprika

½ teaspoon dried basil

Salt and freshly ground black pepper

⅓ cup chicken stock or broth

12 eggs

Pinch of cayenne pepper

16 asparagus spears, cut into 1½-inch lengths and blanched for 1 minute

¾ cup sweet peas (fresh or frozen), blanched 10 seconds

1 large red bell pepper, roasted, cut into ¼-inch strips

2 tablespoons chopped fresh parsley

Preheat the oven to 400°F.

Heat the oil in a skillet over medium heat, add the onion, and cook until soft, about 7 minutes. Add the garlic and stir constantly for 1 minute. Add the tomatoes, balsamic vinegar, paprika, and basil. Season with salt and black pepper and simmer until the tomatoes are soft, about 3 minutes. Increase the heat to high, add the chicken stock, and bring to a boil. Reduce the heat, cover and simmer for 5 minutes. Transfer the sauce to a blender and puree until smooth.

Pour the sauce into a 3-quart ovenproof baking dish. Break 1 egg at a time into a small bowl and slip the eggs into the sauce, distributing them evenly. Season with the cayenne, salt, and black pepper. Arrange the asparagus, peas, and roasted pepper strips decoratively around and between the eggs. Season with salt and black pepper. Bake in the oven until the whites are lightly set and the yolks are still runny, about 10 minutes.

Sprinkle with parsley and serve immediately.

SERVES 6

WINE SUGGESTION: Rosé

WALKING IN THE NEIGHBORHOODS

I love to see the city wake up. Each morning I walk through the different neighborhoods near my own. Sometimes, when I have a lot of energy, I choose the hilly neighborhoods; sometimes, when I want to window shop and take it more leisurely, I choose the more level ones, but I swing my arms and get a good pace going. Either way, when I come home, I always have this smoothie, adding whatever fruit is in season.

MY BREAKFAST SMOOTHIE

¼ cup plain yogurt

¼ cup soy milk

2 teaspoons ground flaxseed

Seasonal fruit of choice

¼ cup freshly squeezed orange juice

2 tablespoons dry protein powder

Put it all in a blender and whir away.

Jalapeño-Jack Scones with Chive Butter

New Zealanders believe they make the best scones in the world. They say it's something about having the lightest touch and incorporating the butter and flour with lots of air. My dear friend and fellow food writer, Lauraine Jacobs, from Auckland, New Zealand, taught me to make scones the way her mother taught her, and I must admit that their technique makes the lightest, flakiest, and most buttery scones I've ever consumed! Most New Zealanders prefer plain scones served warm with sweet jam and soft cream. But I happen to love cheese scones, especially at breakfast. (To make plain scones, increase the butter to 8 tablespoons and omit the cheese. These also make an amazingly light base for strawberry shortcake.)

SCONES

2½ cups flour

Salt

1 tablespoon baking powder

6 tablespoons unsalted butter, chilled

1 cup grated jalapeño-jack cheese (about 4 ounces)

1 cup buttermilk, at room temperature

CHIVE BUTTER

4 tablespoons unsalted butter

3 tablespoons chopped chives

1 clove garlic, minced

Preheat the oven to 400°F.

Make the scones: Sift the flour, 1 teaspoon salt, and baking powder together in a bowl. Using a cheese grater, grate the butter into the flour mixture. Toss together and, with your fingertips, rub the butter into the flour, picking up the mixture and dropping it far above the bowl to incorporate air, until it resembles coarse meal. Add the cheese and toss the mixture together until well mixed.

Add the buttermilk to the dough until it holds together. Form into a mass and roll it quickly on a well-floured surface. Fold it in half and roll again. Repeat, rolling it out to a ³⁄₄-inch thickness. Cut out 10 to 12 scones approximately 1¹⁄₂-inches square.

Place the scones on an ungreased baking sheet and bake until golden, 10 to 12 minutes.

Meanwhile, make the chive butter: Mash together the butter, chives, and garlic. Season with salt.

Serve the warm scones straight from the oven with a small bowl of the chive butter alongside.

MAKES 10 TO 12 SCONES

WINE SUGGESTION: Sparkling wine or spumante

BREAKFAST WITH MY FRIENDS

Summer Fruits in Sweet Spiced Wine (page 268)
Jalapeño-Jack Scones with Chive Butter (page 77)
Baked Eggs with Summer Vegetables (page 74)
My Breakfast Smoothie (page 76)
Bellinis (page 315)

Five-Onion Pizza

You can always go out for a "pie" when you get the urge because great pizzerias exist in every city around the world . . . John's in New York, Chez Panisse in Berkeley, Pizzeria Bianco in Phoenix, Pepe's Pizza in New Haven, Baffetto in Rome, and Pazzia, my favorite in San Francisco. But if you feel like getting your hands in the dough and making your very own pizza, here's a yummy recipe I call "Weir-dough!" When you make it, double or triple the recipe and freeze the dough you don't use in plastic freezer bags. When you want to make a pizza, defrost the dough for an impromptu first course or simple supper. And with so many varieties of onions in the onion family, I make this one with several varieties—leeks, garlic, yellow onions, scallions, and chives. I love the sweet flavors!

> 3 cloves garlic, minced
> 1/4 cup extra-virgin olive oil
> 3/4 cup coarsely grated mozzarella cheese (about 3 ounces)
> 3/4 cup coarsely grated Italian fontina cheese (about 3 ounces)
> 2 leeks, white and 2 inches of the green part, sliced
> 2 yellow onions, thinly sliced
> 6 scallions, white and green parts, thinly sliced
> Salt and freshly ground black pepper
> Favorite Pizza Dough (recipe follows)
> 2 tablespoons chopped fresh chives

Preheat the oven to 500°F. Place a pizza brick on the bottom shelf of the oven.

Combine the garlic and 2 tablespoons of the olive oil and let stand for 30 minutes. Combine the mozzarella and fontina in a bowl.

Heat the remaining 2 tablespoons olive oil in a large skillet over medium heat. Add the leeks and onions and cook, stirring occasionally, until soft, about 20 minutes. Add the scallions and cook, stirring occasionally, until soft, 10 to 15 minutes. Season with salt and pepper.

Divide the pizza dough into 2 round pieces. Do not work the dough too much. Roll and form one piece of dough into a 10- to 11-inch round, 3/8 inch thick. Transfer to a heavily floured pizza peel and brush the dough with the garlic-infused oil leaving a 1/2-inch border. Sprinkle half of the combined cheeses on top of the oil. Top with half of the onion mixture and spread evenly. Sprinkle with salt. Transfer the unbaked pizza directly onto the pizza brick and bake until golden and crisp, about 10 minutes. Repeat with the remaining dough.

When the pizza is done, sprinkle with chives and serve immediately.

MAKES 2 10- TO 11-INCH PIZZAS

WINE SUGGESTION: Pinot Gris, Pinot Grigio; light reds such as Chianti or Sangiovese

Favorite Pizza Dough

3/4 cup plus 2 tablespoons lukewarm water (110°F)

2 teaspoons dry yeast

2 cups bread flour

2 tablespoons olive oil

1 tablespoon milk

1/2 teaspoon salt

Combine 1/4 cup plus 2 tablespoons of the lukewarm water and the yeast in a small bowl. Stir in 1/4 cup of the flour. Let stand for 20 minutes and add the remaining 1 3/4 cups flour, the 1/2 cup lukewarm water, the olive oil, milk, and salt. Mix the dough thoroughly.

Transfer the dough to a floured surface and knead for 10 minutes until soft yet still moist. Place in an oiled bowl, turning once. Cover the bowl with a towel or plastic wrap and place it in a warm spot until the dough has doubled in volume, about 2 hours. Shape the dough.

MAKES ENOUGH FOR 2 10- TO 11-INCH PIZZAS

Moroccan Shellfish Cigars

Around the Eastern and Southern Mediterranean, savory fillings enclosed in phyllo are rolled into cigar shapes, folded into triangles, or shaped into bundles. In Morocco they are called *briouats;* in Tunisia *briks;* in Turkey *bourek* and *boregi;* and in Greece *bourekakia.* By any name, the possibilities for filling these feather-light and melt-in-your-mouth-delicious firsts are nearly limitless. If you want to make these Moroccan Shellfish Cigars into triangles, just cut three-inch strips instead of four-inch strips. Brush one strip lightly with butter and place another one on top. Brush lightly with butter. Place a heaping teaspoon of filling at one end. Fold the corner in to make a triangle, then fold along the line as you would fold a flag. Brush lightly with butter and bake as you would the cigars.

2 tablespoons olive oil

1/4 pound scallops

1/4 pound medium shrimp, peeled

2 cloves garlic, minced

Salt and freshly ground black pepper

1/4 cup finely chopped yellow onion

1 cup peeled, seeded, and chopped tomato (fresh or canned)

3 tablespoons chopped fresh parsley

3 tablespoons chopped fresh cilantro

1 teaspoon ground cumin

1/2 teaspoon sweet paprika

Large pinch of cayenne pepper

Large pinch of saffron threads

1/4 cup fresh bread crumbs

1 stick (4 ounces) butter, melted

1/2 pound phyllo dough

Lemon wedges as a garnish

Heat 1 tablespoon of the oil in a skillet and cook the scallops, shrimp, and half the garlic over low heat for 2 minutes. Season with salt and black pepper. Remove from the pan, place on a work surface and chop coarsely. Reserve in a bowl.

In the same skillet, add the remaining 1 tablespoon oil and the onion and tomato and simmer for 10 minutes. Add the remaining garlic and the parsley, cilantro, cumin, paprika, cayenne, saffron, salt and black pepper. Continue to simmer slowly until the mixture is dry, about 10 minutes. Add the reserved shellfish and the bread crumbs and mix well. Season with salt and black pepper.

Preheat the oven to 375°F. Cut the phyllo lengthwise into 4 equal strips. Place them in one pile and cover with a barely dampened towel until ready to use. Place one piece of phyllo on your work surface and brush lightly with some of the butter. Place another piece of phyllo on top of the first piece and brush lightly with butter. Place a heaping teaspoon of filling along the short end. Fold in the sides and roll, forming a cigar-shape. Brush lightly with butter. Repeat with the remaining phyllo and filling.

Place the cigars evenly apart on an oiled baking sheet and bake in the oven until golden, about 15 minutes.

Serve immediately, garnished with lemon wedges.

MAKES 30; SERVES 6

WINE SUGGESTION: Sauvignon Blanc or Pinot Noir

SHRIMP AND PRAWNS

Whether they're called shrimp or prawns, when you buy them your fishmonger will probably tell you that they are fresh. What he or she *really* means is that they were thawed recently, since almost all shrimp and prawns are frozen directly from the boats prior to sale. Avoid shrimp or prawns that have black spots on their shells; yellow or gritty shells; or shells with dry spots. These all indicate poor quality or damage.

To peel shrimp, use your hands to remove the head from the body; then peel off the remaining shell, leaving the tail flange on, if desired.

To devein (small shrimp or prawns usually don't have to be deveined), use a sharp knife to make a shallow cut along the back of the peeled shrimp and then remove the dark "vein" (actually the intestinal tract, which can give a bitter taste) with the tip of the knife.

My favorite poaching technique is very simple. Bring a frying pan half full of water to a boil over high heat. Salt well. Add the prawns and stir. Bring to a boil and turn off the heat. Let the prawns sit until they are pink and curled. Remove with a slotted spoon.

Straw Potato Cakes with Smoked Salmon and Caviar

Straw potato cakes are kind of an upscale version of the potato pancakes my Lithuanian grandmother and later my mother used to make for us every Friday night. My mother would tell us that it was important to let the grated potatoes turn brown before cooking them. Then she would stand at the stove and make them, one after another, serving them to us hot from the pan and topped with cottage cheese. We kept eating them, one after another! This version topped with smoked salmon and caviar is a great first course for a dinner party.

2¼ pounds baking potatoes

6 tablespoons unsalted butter

Salt and freshly ground black pepper

½ cup crème fraîche or sour cream

8 ounces thinly sliced smoked salmon

1 ounce caviar (American sturgeon, Beluga, Osetra, or Sevruga) or
    salmon roe

1 tablespoon chopped fresh chives or 1 scallion, white and green parts,
    thinly sliced

Peel the potatoes and cut them on a mandoline or by hand into fine julienne strips. Place the potatoes in a large bowl and cover them with several changes of cold water until the water is clear and no longer milky. Let them soak for 1 hour.

Melt the butter in a saucepan over medium heat. Let sit for 20 minutes. Spoon the foam off the top and discard. Spoon the deep-yellow clear butterfat into a clean bowl. Discard the whey that remains on the bottom.

Drain the potatoes and spin them dry in a salad spinner. Toss with salt and pepper. Melt 2 tablespoons of butter in a 10-inch nonstick skillet over medium-high heat until it sizzles when you touch a potato to it. Add one-third of the potatoes and press

lightly with a smaller lid or spatula to form a flat cake to fill the bottom of the pan. Cook the potato cake until golden on the bottom, 5 to 8 minutes. Keep the heat high enough so that you hear a gentle sizzle and, several times during the cooking, move the pan back and forth. The potatoes are ready to flip when the aroma changes from steamy to nutty. Place a flat lid or plate over the skillet and invert the pan. Carefully slide the potato cake back into the pan. Continue to cook the cake for another 8 minutes or so, until it is thoroughly browned and crisp on the second side. When it is done, transfer it to a warm paper towel–lined plate and place in a warm oven. Repeat the process, making two more potato cakes.

Place the crème fraîche in a bowl. To thin slightly, add 1 tablespoon water. Season with salt and pepper.

Cut each straw potato cake into 4 wedges (if the cakes have cooled, place them on a baking sheet on the top shelf of a 500°F oven and heat them until crisp and golden, 6 to 10 minutes). Place two wedges on each plate. Top the cakes with the salmon, drizzle with crème fraîche, dollop with caviar, and sprinkle with chives. Serve immediately.

SERVES 6

WINE SUGGESTION: Dry sparkling wine, champagne, or Chardonnay

---

"What is the city but the people?"

WILLIAM SHAKESPEARE

Scallop Seviche with Tomatoes, Hot Peppers, and Cilantro

Latin Americans "cook" raw scallops in freshly squeezed lime juice and then toss them with cherry tomatoes, thin strips of bell pepper, jalapeño chiles, and cilantro (diced avocado can also be added). They call it seviche, and I'm a fool for it. It's hot; it's tart; and it's refreshing! Serve as a first-course salad with hot, crispy corn tortilla chips. The most important thing I can tell you about seviche or any recipe using fresh fish is to be sure to buy the very freshest fish from your local trustworthy fishmonger.

1 pound very fresh sea or bay
  scallops
3/4 cup fresh lime juice
3/4 pound cherry tomatoes
  (assorted colors), halved
1/2 red bell pepper, seeded and
  cut into 1-inch strips
1/2 yellow bell pepper, seeded and
  cut into 1-inch strips

2 jalapeño chiles, seeded and minced
1/2 cup thinly sliced scallions
2 cloves garlic, minced
1/3 cup coarsely chopped fresh
  cilantro
3 tablespoons extra-virgin olive oil
Salt and freshly ground black pepper
Lime wedges as a garnish
Cilantro sprigs as a garnish

Remove the small white muscle from the side of each scallop. If you are using sea scallops, slice them horizontally into 1/4-inch slices. If you are using bay scallops, leave them whole. Place the scallops in a bowl with the lime juice, mix together, and let sit for 1 hour.

After 1 hour, add the tomatoes, bell peppers, jalapeños, scallions, garlic, cilantro, and olive oil. Season to taste with salt and black pepper, and mix well. Serve, garnished with lime wedges and cilantro sprigs. This dish can be made up to 6 hours in advance (garnish with the lime wedges and cilantro sprigs just before serving).

SERVES 6

WINE SUGGESTION: Gewürztraminer

SCALLOPS

The scallop shell has been used in art and architecture from earliest times. Aphrodite, the Greek goddess of love and beauty, was said to have ridden over the Aegean sea on a scallop shell and onto the island of Cythera in a scallop carriage.

Of the roughly 400 different species of scallops, only about 12 come to market. Among these, both bay and sea scallops are commonly available, equally sweet, and virtually interchangeable (though cooking times will vary accordingly according to their size). Bay scallops are small, $1/2$ to $3/4$ inch in diameter; sea scallops are larger, at 1 to $1^1/4$ inches in diameter. Though the whole scallop is edible, we eat only the tender adductor muscle.

So-called "day-boat scallops" refer to scallops that are harvested by fishermen who go out for a single day and return to market with fresh, untreated shellfish. (Scallop boats normally go far offshore and fish for several days, necessitating various methods of preserving the highly-perishable scallop, including bleaching.) A day-boat scallop can be identified by its ivory and coral color; bleached scallops are very white.

Oysters with Champagne Mignonette

I don't think there's a better first course than a platter of icy cold, freshly shucked oysters. I remember when I was growing up in Massachusetts, the only oysters available were big fat ones called Blue Point. But now there are so many other varieties available— Kumamoto, Hog Island, Quilcene, Belon, Wellfleet, Malpeque, Olympia, Apalachicola, to name just a few. No matter what variety, I love to serve them with a glass of something bubbly. The best accompaniment for oysters in my estimation is a pungent little sauce called mignonette made with champagne or sparkling wine that is mixed with champagne vinegar, chopped shallots, and freshly cracked black pepper. I was first introduced to mignonette years ago while traveling in France. Then, when I worked at Chez Panisse, I used to have to open dozens of oysters and make this sauce daily. Serve oysters on a bed of rock salt with fresh rye bread slathered with sweet butter.

> 2 dozen fresh oysters in the shell
> 1/2 cup champagne or sparkling wine
> 2 to 3 tablespoons champagne vinegar
> 1 shallot, minced
> Salt and freshly ground black pepper
> 6 lemon wedges as a garnish
> Sprigs of flat-leaf Italian parsley as a garnish

Open the oysters and discard the top shell. Place them, in a single layer, on a bed of rock salt.

In a small bowl, whisk together the champagne, champagne vinegar, and shallots. Season to taste with salt and pepper. Place in a small bowl and serve it alongside the oysters. Garnish with lemon wedges and parsley.

SERVES 6

WINE SUGGESTION: Champagne or Sauvignon Blanc

ON THE HALF SHELL

When I'm going to make a dish like Oysters with Champagne Mignonette, which is served raw on the half shell, I always look for the freshest oysters. But I never ask my fishmonger, "Did these come in today?" because I know he or she will always say, "Yes, of course." Instead I ask, "*When* did these come in?" I also ask to see and smell the oysters. They should be tightly closed and smell briny and salty, like the sea. Use them as quickly as possible, preferably the same day. (If you are storing them, keep them in a bowl or mesh bag in the refrigerator, loosely covered with a moistened kitchen towel, for up to 24 hours.)

As with all mollusks (this includes clams, scallops, mussels, and oysters), it's best not to gather oysters in the wild unless you are really sure that the area is safe and impeccably clean. Mollusks filter the water they live in through their bodies; if there are pathogens in the water, they will end up in the shellfish. So-called legal mollusks are grown in licensed areas, which undergo regular inspection. The people who harvest them have to tag them with their names and the area from which they were taken.

To clean oysters, using a good stiff brush, wash and brush them under the coldest water that runs from your tap.

To shuck oysters, hold the oyster in a folded kitchen towel and then slip a sturdy, short oyster knife (which has a strong, pointed blade and a shield to protect your hand) into the hinge end, pop the top open, and run the knife along the edge until the top comes off. Then cut the tendon that holds the oyster to the shell. To finish, flip the oyster in the shell to show its smooth underside.

Yakitori with Red and Green Peppers

Yakitori is a kind of Japanese shish kebab; that is, meat and vegetables threaded onto metal or wooden skewers and grilled. When I am in Los Angeles, I love to eat at a little neighborhood restaurant called Yakitoria, where they specialize in everything made on skewers: meat, vegetable, or fruit. Serve yakitori either as a first course or as a main course with a bowl of rice, a nice pot of green tea, and pickles on the side.

> 5 chicken thighs (about 1¼ pounds), boned and skinned
> ½ green bell pepper
> ½ red bell pepper
> Salt
> 6 tablespoons Japanese soy sauce or shoyu
> ¼ cup sake or sherry
> 2 teaspoons finely grated fresh ginger
> 3 tablespoons sugar

Soak 12 5- to 7-inch bamboo skewers in water for 30 minutes. Cut the chicken into 1-inch chunks. Core, seed, and cut the bell peppers into 1-inch squares.

Thread the chicken and bell peppers onto the skewers, distributing them evenly and pushing to one end of the skewer. Season with salt.

In a saucepan, bring the soy sauce, sake, ginger, and sugar to a boil over medium-high heat. Reduce the heat and simmer for 5 minutes. Remove from the heat.

Preheat an outdoor grill, a broiler, or an indoor cast-iron ridged grill (if you are using an indoor cast-iron grill, place it on medium heat for 10 minutes before using). Grill or broil the yakitori skewers, turning occasionally, until the meat is golden but not thoroughly cooked, 10 to 12 minutes. Brush with the sauce on all sides and continue to grill for 1 to 2 minutes. Repeat, brushing the yakitori skewers with the sauce again and grill for another 1 to 2 minutes.

Place on a platter and serve.

SERVES 6 AS AN APPETIZER

WINE SUGGESTION: Chardonnay or Merlot

JAPANTOWN MENU

Your Favorite Sushi

Miso Soup with Edamame (page 148)

Yakitori with Red and Green Peppers (page 92)

Japanese Pickled Vegetable Salad (page 133)

Foraging in the City

Some people head to the supermarket with a shopping list. I am a forager. I always have an eye out for the little, out-of-the-way bakery, fishmonger, cheese shop, specialty market, or farmers' market in one of the neighborhoods. I go without a menu in mind and search with no end but to find what looks really good and sets off a signal in me. A special basket of greengage plums inspires a tart; heirloom tomatoes make me think of homemade pizza; some day-boat scallops conjure a seviche.

I also believe in keeping things simple, and sometimes the supermarket, where I can buy everything under the sun at any time and in any season, is the answer. But sometimes it's not. To me, the amazing thing about living in a modern city is that so many resources and ingredients are available to us, not that they are available year-round. Selecting food at the peak of its season and going to small vendors whom you get to know and who get to know you can make you feel that you live in a richer environment and a grander time. And I love the feeling that my city's streets are not so much filled with impersonal skyscrapers as street-level shops teeming with noise, fresh ingredients, great-smelling food, and interesting people.

This doesn't mean that you have to scour the city or go to five different places to assemble a family meal. It does mean that you have to learn to see your city—even your really big city—as a mass of small, hidden treasures awaiting your discovery. And it means that you should be able to find a few places where you can reliably get the best of anything.

You'll need: a butcher; baker; fishmonger; farmers' market or vegetable stand; wine merchant; and a place for flowers, candles, and linens. You might also want to find a few other special places, like the farm I go to about an hour out of the city that grows and sells superb beans and peaches.

How do you find the top places? Ask around; listen; be on the alert for information; and relax, you've got time. This should be fun. Find one today, another next week. Once you have found your special sources, cultivate them; go back often; be gracious; give them as much business as you can. And ask questions. What is the appropriate cut of meat for this dish? What is the best way to cook this vegetable? How do you clean this fish? What wine will go with this dish? As you begin to establish yourself as a "regular," you will be rewarded with the choicest selections, insider recommendations, and special things saved for you. Heed the advice of the experts you have found. And keep looking.

Garden Greens with Tomatoes, Lime, Olives, and Cilantro

Mexican restaurants and markets abound in the Mission District of the city. It's a lively neighborhood and close enough to my own that I can ride my motor scooter there. On one of my foraging ventures recently, I discovered a great market where I can pick up a dozen fresh, hot, flour tortillas, sweet red cherry tomatoes, a big bunch of cilantro, and lots of limes for a very reasonable price. Last time I was there, I found 20 limes for a dollar! I zoomed home and whipped up margaritas, quesadillas, and this tasty, zestful salad.

    5 tablespoons extra-virgin olive oil
    2 tablespoons fresh lime juice
    1 tablespoon grated lime zest
    2 cloves garlic, minced
    1 jalapeño chile, seeded and minced
    Salt and freshly ground black pepper
    10 to 12 cups assorted baby salad greens
    2 cups cherry tomatoes (preferably a variety of colors), halved
    1 cup Picholine, Lucques, Kalamata, or Niçoise olives, pitted and halved
    ½ cup fresh cilantro leaves

In a bowl, whisk together the olive oil, lime juice, lime zest, garlic, and jalapeño. Season with salt and black pepper.

Place the salad greens, cherry tomatoes, olives, and cilantro in a large bowl. Add the dressing and toss together. Place the greens on a platter and serve immediately.

SERVES 6

WINE SUGGESTION: Pinot Gris

Cherry Tomato Salad with Herbed Feta

Every time I teach a class lately, someone asks, "What kind of salt do you like to use?" Years ago when I cooked at Chez Panisse, I was introduced to kosher salt and I never looked back. Kosher salt melts much faster than other table or sea salt, contains no chemicals, has larger granules so they are easier to regulate when adding a pinch of salt to a dish, and the taste is better. I like salt; it brings out the flavors in a dish. That is probably why I like feta, the sheep or goat's milk cheese traditionally made in Greece. The salty brine in which it's stored helps the cheese retain its young, fresh flavor, as you'll see in this wonderful salad.

$1/2$ pound feta

2 tablespoons chopped fresh basil

1 tablespoon chopped fresh mint

1 tablespoon chopped fresh chives

1 teaspoon chopped fresh oregano

1 teaspoon chopped fresh thyme

$1^1/2$ pounds cherry tomatoes (in a colorful variety of red, orange, yellow plum, green), halved

Kosher salt

$1/4$ cup extra-virgin olive oil

2 tablespoons lemon juice

1 teaspoon grated lemon zest

Freshly ground black pepper

Basil, mint, oregano, and thyme sprigs as a garnish

Crumble the feta coarsely in a bowl. Add the basil, mint, chives, oregano, and thyme and mix together until all of the herbs are stuck to the cheese. Reserve.

Place the cherry tomatoes on a serving platter. Season with salt.

In a small bowl, whisk together the olive oil, lemon juice, and lemon zest. Season with salt and pepper.

To serve, drizzle the dressing over the tomatoes. Scatter the cheese on top and garnish with the herb sprigs. Serve immediately.

SERVES 6

WINE SUGGESTION: Sauvignon Blanc

HERBS ON THE TERRACE

I love to use fresh herbs when I'm cooking, but living in the city, I don't have room for a garden. So I have about 15 very large pots on my balcony that I fill with herbs and flowers and tend with all the dedication and pleasure of any country gardener. The pots surround my little table where I like to sit on sunny days, and fill the air with their incredible scents.

Almost any dish, no matter how simple, can be made more flavorful when you give it that freshness that just-picked herbs impart. Fresh thyme stirred into the stockpot; rosemary sprigs placed in the cavity of a roast chicken; a little oregano added to a fresh tomato sauce. Plus, there is the incalculable satisfaction of growing something yourself and going out to enjoy your garden every morning, and the sensory delights of beautiful and good-smelling plants.

I like to group my herbs according to how much water they need. Thyme, rosemary, and oregano need very little water; parsley seems to need more, so I put it in pots that I water more often. To add color, I like to mix in flowers like pansies, violets, lavender, Gerber daisies, nasturtiums, and alyssum. To give height, I have some tall branch-poles on which I train rosemary and lavender.

In choosing which herbs to grow, I'm greatly influenced by local weather conditions (some things just don't grow well in this city), but also by my cooking needs. I'll try more exotic herbs, things that are tougher to grow, like lemon verbena, garlic chives, dill, or cilantro. But I always have the following:

Basil	Oregano	Rosemary	Tarragon
Chives	Parsley (flat-	Sage	Thyme
Mint	leaf variety)	Savory	

Depending on where you live and how much sun you get, you can grow most herbs year-round whether it is in your garden or in a windowsill pot. You'll have to experiment in your particular environment. In the right climate, rosemary will grow to a bush and you'll grow enough basil to make pesto. But sometimes you just need a few leaves of basil for a tomato salad, and almost any summer climate can handle a plant or two.

"To feel, amid the city's jar,

That there abides a peace of thine,

Man did not make, and can not mar."

MATTHEW ARNOLD

Roasted Pepper Salad
with Eggplant Croutons

This is really two dishes in one. The pepper salad could be an offering on a summer buffet and the eggplant croutons a simple first course with a glass of wine. Or, as I love them, together!

1 medium eggplant, peeled and
    cut into 1-inch chunks
6 tablespoons extra-virgin olive oil
6 tablespoons red wine vinegar
6 sprigs thyme
2 bay leaves
6 cloves garlic, peeled and halved
3 red bell peppers
3 yellow bell peppers
3 anchovy fillets

$\frac{1}{3}$ cup Niçoise or Kalamata olives,
    pitted and chopped
$\frac{1}{4}$ cup minced red onion
3 tablespoons capers, rinsed and
    chopped
Salt and freshly ground black
    pepper
$\frac{1}{2}$ loaf coarse-textured Italian or
    French bread
$\frac{1}{3}$ cup fresh flat-leaf parsley leaves

Place the eggplant in a large skillet with 5 tablespoons of the olive oil and vinegar, and the thyme, bay leaves, and garlic. Add enough water to come almost to the level of the eggplant. Bring to a boil over high heat, reduce the heat and simmer, stirring occasionally, for 10 minutes. Remove from the heat, cover, and let cool in the pan.

Place the bell peppers directly over a gas flame and turn occasionally until black on all sides. Alternatively, cut the bell peppers in half lengthwise and remove the stems, seeds, and ribs, place cut side down on a baking sheet; and broil until the skin is blackened, about 10 minutes. Transfer the peppers to a plastic bag, close tightly, and let cool for 10 minutes. Remove the skin by scraping with a knife. Cut the peppers into 1-inch-wide strips and place in a bowl.

Place the anchovies in a bowl of cold water and let soak for 10 minutes. Remove and pat dry with paper towels and then mince.

When the eggplant has cooled, remove the thyme and bay leaves and discard. Using a slotted spoon, transfer the eggplant and garlic from the skillet to a food processor and finely chop or pulse. Place in a bowl and stir in the olives, red onion, capers, and anchovies. Season with salt, pepper, and up to 2 more teaspoons vinegar if needed.

Cut the bread into ½-inch slices. Toast or grill the bread until golden. Cut into 2- to 3-inch pieces and spread each piece with the eggplant mixture.

Toss the roasted peppers with the remaining 1 tablespoon olive oil and remaining 1 teaspoon vinegar. Season with salt and pepper. Toss with the parsley leaves. Place on a platter and arrange the eggplant croutons around the edges. Serve.

SERVES 6

WINE SUGGESTION: Pinot Grigio, Sauvignon Blanc, Beaujolais, or Pinot Noir

Autumn Cheddar, Apple, and Walnut Salad

Growing up in New England included an obligatory day of apple picking every fall. Sometimes we went to my grandfather's farm; other times we went to my mother's favorite orchard. My sister, Nancy, and I used to see how many apples we could pack into a bushel basket. The contest was fun, but carrying the basket to the car was another story.

3/4 cup walnut halves

1 cup apple juice

3 tablespoons extra-virgin olive oil

2 tablespoons apple cider vinegar

Salt and freshly ground black pepper

2 crisp red apples (Jonagold, McIntosh, Red Beauty, Gravenstein)

10 to 12 cups baby salad greens

3-ounce chunk aged sharp cheddar

Preheat the oven to 375°F. Place the walnuts on a baking sheet and bake until the nuts are light golden and hot to the touch, 5 to 7 minutes. Reserve.

Place the apple juice in a saucepan over medium-high heat. Reduce the juice to 3 tablespoons. Let cool.

In a bowl, whisk together the reduced apple juice, olive oil, and apple cider vinegar. Season with salt and pepper.

Just before serving, cut the apples in half and core. Cut into thin slices. Toss the salad greens with the vinaigrette, walnuts, and apples. With a cheese shaver or vegetable peeler, shave thin shards of the cheese onto the top of the salad. Toss gently and serve immediately.

SERVES 6

WINE SUGGESTION: Chardonnay

Roasted Beet, Avocado, and Watercress Salad

Why is it that when we think of salad, our thoughts go directly to lettuce? Must be a throwback from when we were kids. When I was growing up, we had salads every night, all year long. And in the winter months in New England, the pickings were pretty slim. I distinctly remember watery iceberg lettuce; mealy, flavorless, hard, pink tomatoes; and waxy cucumbers. But my dad still wanted his salad! It must have broken my mother's heart, as she was not only a fantastic cook but also an avid gardener. Despite all this, winter can be one of the best times to make salad using seasonal vegetables and greens for something completely different.

1½ pounds medium beets (red or gold), washed

5 tablespoons extra-virgin olive oil

½ cup pecan halves

2 tablespoons orange juice

1½ tablespoons sherry vinegar

1 teaspoon finely grated orange zest

Salt and freshly ground black pepper

½ small red onion, peeled and cut into ¼-inch rings

2 avocados, peeled and sliced into ¼-inch slices

2 bunches watercress, stems discarded

Preheat the oven to 375°F. Place the beets in a shallow baking dish and drizzle with 1 tablespoon of the olive oil and 1 tablespoon water. Roll the beets to coat them. Cover the beets with foil and bake until tender when pierced with a knife, 60 to 80 minutes. Allow them to cool enough to handle. Peel the beets and cut into thin ¼-inch slices and reserve.

Preheat the oven to 375°F. Place the pecans on a baking sheet and bake in the oven until light golden and hot to the touch, 5 to 7 minutes. Reserve.

Meanwhile, in a bowl, whisk together the remaining 4 tablespoons olive oil, orange juice, sherry vinegar, and orange zest. Season with salt and pepper. Toss half of the vinaigrette with the beets and place the beets on a platter. Top with the onion and avocado slices.

Toss the watercress and pecans with the remaining vinaigrette and place on top of the salad. Serve immediately.

SERVES 6

WINE SUGGESTION: Sauvignon Blanc or Grüner Veltliner

SLICING AN AVOCADO

Cut the avocado in half lengthwise, twisting the two pieces to separate the halves. Tap the blade of your knife into the pit to lodge the blade in the pit. Twist the blade and remove the pit. With a large spoon, scoop out the pulp. Discard the pit and skin. Cut the avocado into 1/4-inch slices.

Orzo Salad with Capers, Corn, Red Onion, and Peppers

I am always looking for great picnic food. Whether I am going out on the Bay with friends for a day of sailing or to Golden Gate Park, I want something that is quick and simple to prepare, something that gets rave reviews, and something that is easy to transport. And to be perfectly honest, I can usually make it with whatever I might have left over in my refrigerator and what's in my balcony garden. For this orzo dish, sometimes I toss in some smoked, diced chicken; chopped basil, oregano, or summer savory; a few pitted chopped green or black olives; or even diced, seeded cucumbers.

2 quarts water	3 scallions, white and green parts, thinly sliced
Salt	
1½ cups orzo	1 small red bell pepper, cut into ¼-inch dice
5 tablespoons extra-virgin olive oil	
2 ears corn, husks and silk removed	1 small yellow bell pepper, cut into ¼-inch dice
¼ cup lemon juice	¼ cup capers, rinsed
1 teaspoon grated lemon zest	2 tablespoons chopped fresh parsley
Freshly ground black pepper	
1 small red onion, cut into ¼-inch dice	Lemon wedges as a garnish
	Parsley leaves as a garnish

In a large saucepan, bring the water and 1 tablespoon salt to a boil. Add the orzo and cook until tender, about 5 minutes. Drain the orzo and immediately toss with 1 tablespoon of the olive oil. Let cool completely in the refrigerator.

Bring a large saucepan of salted water to a boil. Add the corn and cook, turning occasionally, until done, 5 minutes. Remove and let cool. Using a knife, cut the kernels off the cob and reserve. Discard the cobs.

In a large bowl, whisk together the remaining 4 tablespoons olive oil, lemon juice, and lemon zest. Season with salt and pepper. Add the corn, red onion, scallions, red and yellow bell peppers, capers, and parsley. Add the orzo and stir together. Season with salt and pepper.

To serve, place the salad in a serving bowl and garnish with lemon wedges and parsley leaves.

SERVES 6

WINE SUGGESTION: Sauvignon Blanc

> *"In the main towns of the French provinces, markets run by the municipalities still supply every local fruit, vegetable, cheese, and sausage as it is ready for the eating, and in an odd way these places triumph over the new supermarkets, at least in their ever-changing variety and fresh delights."*
>
> M.F.K. FISHER

Artichoke, Endive, and Arugula Salad

Can you believe that artichokes are actually thorny blossoms? During the spring, artichokes are most prolific. A good year for the artichoke means that there is also a second harvest, usually a smaller one, in autumn. That would be a good time to serve this salad. If you're wondering why there isn't a wine suggestion, it's because artichokes are one of the most difficult ingredients to pair with wine. If you must, try Sauvignon Blanc.

2 lemons

12 small artichokes or 4 medium
    artichokes

4 bay leaves

6 cloves garlic, 5 peeled and
    thinly sliced and 1 minced

1/3 cup olive oil

Salt

3 heads endive

1/4 cup extra-virgin olive oil

2 tablespoons lemon juice

Freshly ground black pepper

4 cups arugula leaves

3-ounce chunk Parmigiano-
    Reggiano cheese

With a vegetable peeler, remove the peel from the lemons; set aside. Have ready a large bowl of water to which you have added the juice of 1 lemon. Cut off the top half of the artichokes including all of the prickly leaf points. Remove the tough outer leaves of the artichoke until you get to the very light green leaves. Pare the stem to reveal the light green center. If using large artichokes, cut in half lengthwise, then scoop out the prickly chokes and discard. Cut in half again. As each is cut, place in the lemon water.

Drain the artichokes and place them in a saucepan with the juice of the remaining lemon, lemon peel, bay leaves, sliced garlic, and olive oil. Season with salt. Add water just to cover. Cover with a piece of parchment and weight the parchment with a small plate that fits inside the pan. Bring to a boil over medium-high heat, then reduce the heat and simmer for 5 minutes. Turn off the heat and let cool completely, about 1 hour. Drain the artichokes and halve the small artichokes. Reserve.

Cut about 1½ inches off one head of endive on a sharp diagonal. Turn the endive and continue to make diagonal cuts so that the pieces of endive are all about the same size. Repeat with the remaining endive.

In a small bowl, whisk together the 2 tablespoons extra-virgin olive oil, lemon juice, and minced garlic. Season with salt and pepper.

Place the artichokes, endive, and arugula in a bowl. Toss with the dressing and place on a platter. With a cheese shaver or vegetable peeler, shave thin shards of the cheese onto the top. Serve immediately.

SERVES 6

DAY AT THE BEACH

Artichoke, Endive, and Arugula Salad (page 109)
Clam and Mussel Boil with Corn and Red Potatoes (page 222)
Cedar-Planked Lemon Salmon with Dill (page 214)
Ginger Crisps (page 291)

Warm Grilled Fennel Salad

I know how difficult timing can be when you are entertaining. But there is something about a salad like this when it is served warm, especially straight from the grill when the flavors are at their peak. My secret is to have everything ready in advance. (Of course, you can always serve this salad at room temperature and it will still be delicious!) The best way to crush fennel seeds is with a mortar and pestle; or wrap them in a cotton or linen kitchen towel and tap them with the handle of a chef's knife or the bottom of a heavy pan (or even a hammer).

> 4 large bulbs fennel
>
> Salt
>
> 7 tablespoons extra-virgin olive oil or fennel oil
>
> ¼ cup lemon juice
>
> 1 tablespoon grated lemon zest
>
> ½ teaspoon crushed fennel seeds
>
> Freshly ground black pepper
>
> 1 tablespoon chopped fresh flat-leaf parsley
>
> 3-ounce chunk young Pecorino, or Parmigiano-Reggiano cheese
>
> 6 lemon wedges as a garnish

Preheat an outdoor grill, a broiler, or an indoor cast-iron ridged grill pan (if you are using an indoor cast-iron grill, place it on medium heat for 10 minutes before serving the salad).

Trim the bottoms and tops off the fennel. If any of the outer leaves are damaged, remove or trim them. Cut the fennel bulbs into sixths so that the core holds them together. If there are any feathery bright green tops, chop them and reserve 2 tablespoons.

Bring a saucepan of salted water to a boil. Add the fennel and simmer until crisp-tender, 3 to 4 minutes. Let cool.

In a large bowl, whisk together 6 tablespoons of the olive oil, the lemon juice, lemon zest, and fennel seeds. Season with salt and pepper.

Brush the fennel on all sides with the remaining 1 tablespoon olive oil. Grill, turning occasionally, until golden on all sides, from 10 minutes. Add to the dressing with the parsley and chopped fennel tops. Toss together. Season with salt and pepper. Place on a serving platter and with a cheese shaver or vegetable peeler, shave shards of Pecorino on top. Serve garnished with lemon wedges.

SERVES 6

WINE SUGGESTION: Italian whites, such as Arneis, Est! Est!! Est!!!, or Greco di Tufo

"If you are lucky enough to have lived in Paris as a young man,

then wherever you go for the rest of your life, it stays with you,

for Paris is a moveable feast."

ERNEST HEMINGWAY

Escarole Salad with Anchovy Vinaigrette and Garlic Croutons

One of the best ways to temper anchovies' saltiness is to soak them in a cold water bath, then drain them, dry with paper towels, and mince. A whole new kettle of fish, so to speak.

1/4 pound stale peasant bread, crusts removed

5 tablespoons extra-virgin olive oil

3 cloves garlic, minced

Salt and freshly ground black pepper

6 anchovy fillets

3 tablespoons chopped fresh parsley

1 shallot, minced

2 tablespoons red wine vinegar

1 head escarole, torn into 2-inch pieces

Preheat the oven to 400°F. Tear the bread into 3/4-inch pieces or cut into 3/4-inch cubes. Place in a single layer on a baking sheet. Warm 2 tablespoons of the olive oil in a small saucepan. Add half of the garlic and turn off the heat immediately. Pour the oil over the bread and toss with salt and pepper. Bake until golden and crisp, tossing occasionally, 10 to 15 minutes.

Place the anchovies in a bowl of cold water. Soak for 10 minutes. Remove and pat dry with paper towels, then mince.

In a large bowl, whisk together the anchovies, remaining 3 tablespoons olive oil, remaining garlic, parsley, shallot, and vinegar. Season with salt and pepper. Add the escarole and toss together.

Place the salad in a serving bowl and garnish with the croutons. Serve immediately.

SERVES 6

WINE SUGGESTION: Prosecco

Spicy Bulgur and Lentil Salad

I believe that whenever you have guests, everyone arrives hungry. So I always try to have something to eat right when my guests arrive. This is a great make-ahead, gutsy autumn or winter starter that can be addictive, especially if you have a weakness for cumin.

³/₄ cup small French lentils	3 tablespoons lemon juice
¹/₂ cup bulgur, rinsed and drained	2 teaspoons ground cumin
¹/₄ cup extra-virgin olive oil	1 clove garlic, minced
1 small red onion, minced	¹/₂ teaspoon crushed red pepper
¹/₂ cup chopped fresh flat-leaf parsley	Salt and freshly ground black pepper
5 scallions, white and green, thinly sliced	3 heads baby romaine lettuce, leaves separated

Place the lentils in a saucepan and add enough water to cover by two inches. Bring to a boil, then simmer over medium-low heat until tender, 15 to 25 minutes. If any liquid remains, drain and discard. Pour the hot lentils over the bulgur and mix thoroughly. Cover and let stand until the bulgur becomes soft, about 1 hour.

Meanwhile, heat the olive oil in a large skillet over medium heat. Add the onion and cook until light golden, 10 to 12 minutes. Pour the onion and oil from the pan into the bulgur-lentil mixture. Add the parsley, scallions, lemon juice, cumin, garlic, and crushed red pepper. Season with salt and pepper and additional lemon juice if needed; mix well.

To serve, place the salad in the center of a plate and use the romaine leaves as a scoop to serve.

SERVES 6

WINE SUGGESTION: Chianti or a red Rhône

Dried Plum, Fennel, and Manchego Salad with Prosciutto

This is another great winter salad, pairing dried plums with licorice-flavored, paper-thin slices of shaved fennel, homemade fennel oil, and salty manchego cheese and prosciutto. What a combination!

2 teaspoons lemon juice

15 pitted dried plums or prunes

1 bulb fennel

2 bunches frisée

3 tablespoons fennel oil (recipe follows)

Salt and freshly ground black pepper

4-ounce chunk manchego cheese

6 thin slices prosciutto, Serrano ham, or duck prosciutto

Bring a small pot of water to a boil. Add 1 teaspoon of the lemon juice. Remove from the heat, add the dried plums, and set aside for 30 minutes. Halve the dried plums.

Cut the top and stem end off the fennel, leaving the bulb intact. Cut the fennel in half lengthwise. Using a sharp knife or a mandolin, cut the fennel into paper-thin slices.

Place the fennel and frisée in a bowl. Add the fennel oil, remaining 1 teaspoon lemon juice, and salt and pepper; toss together.

Distribute the frisée and fennel on serving plates. Distribute the dried plums on top. Shave the Manchego onto the salad. Cut each slice of prosciutto into two lengthwise pieces; scatter over the cheese. Serve.

SERVES 6

WINE SUGGESTION: Riesling, Beaujolais, or Sangiovese

Fennel Oil

3 tablespoons fennel seeds
1 cup extra-virgin olive oil

Heat a dry skillet over medium heat. Add the fennel seeds and shake the pan constantly for 15 to 30 seconds. Do not allow the seeds to turn brown.

Grind the fennel seeds in a grinder or a mortar and pestle until coarsely ground.

Place the olive oil and fennel seeds in a jar and shake. Let sit for 7 days, then strain. Store in a covered glass jar for up to 6 months in a cool, dark place.

MAKES 1 CUP

Celebration Salad of Endive, Crème Fraîche, and Caviar

The best time to make this salad is around Christmas or New Year's when salmon caviar comes into season. In the weeks just before the holidays, I will make several trips to the European specialty markets in the city that carry a wide variety, looking for caviar of the best quality in terms of freshness and flavor, at the best price. Salmon caviar looks very different from the much more expensive beluga, sevruga, or osetra varieties, which are the lightly salted roe or eggs from sturgeon; salmon caviar looks like beautiful, small coral-colored pearls. You can see that this salad is pretty simple, and focuses on the best, freshest ingredients—my favorite way to cook.

  8 heads Belgian endive
  1 cup crème fraîche, at room temperature
  2 teaspoons lemon juice
  Salt and freshly ground black pepper
  2 ounces salmon caviar
  2 tablespoons very thinly sliced fresh chives as a garnish
  1 bunch chervil or 1 small bunch frisée, ends trimmed as a garnish

Trim the bottom off each endive and discard. Remove any leaves that are loose and place in a bowl. Cut off approximately ¼ inch of the end of the endive and continue to remove the whole leaves. Place in a bowl with the others. Repeat with the remaining endive.

In another bowl, stir together the crème fraîche and lemon juice. Season with salt and pepper.

To serve, toss the endive with the crème fraîche mixture. Place on a platter. Spoon the caviar onto the endive. Garnish with the chives and chervil and serve immediately.

SERVES 6

WINE SUGGESTION: Brut champagnes or rosé

Radicchio, Arugula, Golden Raisin, and Pine Nut Salad

Rome, along with Venice, New York, Sydney, and, of course, San Francisco top my list of favorite cities. This salad comes from Rome. It has the *agrodolce* or sweet and sour combination that the Italians, especially in the south, love so much. This salad is great to make during the winter months when all of these ingredients are at their prime.

> 1/4 cup pine nuts
> 1 large bulb fennel
> 1 medium head radicchio, torn into 2-inch pieces
> 1 large bunch arugula, stems removed
> 3 blood oranges or seedless oranges
> 1/4 cup fresh orange juice
> 3 tablespoons extra-virgin olive oil
> 1 1/2 tablespoons red wine vinegar
> Salt and freshly ground black pepper
> 1/3 cup golden raisins or sultanas

Warm a small skillet over medium heat. Add the pine nuts and cook, stirring and shaking the pan constantly, until the pine nuts are light golden, 2 minutes. Remove the nuts from the pan immediately.

Cut the stem end and top off the fennel, leaving the bulb intact. Cut the fennel lengthwise. Using a sharp knife or a mandolin, cut the fennel into paper-thin slices.

Combine the fennel, radicchio, and arugula in a bowl and refrigerate.

Finely grate 1 teaspoon orange zest; reserve. Cut the top and bottom off the oranges. Place one of the cut sides down on a work surface. Starting at the top and following the contour of the orange down, cut off the skin, leaving no white pith remaining. Cut the peeled orange into slices. Reserve. Repeat with the remaining oranges.

In a bowl, whisk together the orange juice, olive oil, red wine vinegar and reserved orange zest. Season with salt and pepper. Add the raisins.

Toss the reserved salad greens with the vinaigrette. Place on individual serving plates and garnish with the orange slices and pine nuts. Serve immediately.

SERVES 6

WINE SUGGESTION: Pinot Grigio or Sauvignon Blanc

BUTCHER, BAKER, CANDLESTICK MAKER

I don't know when I first started to see the city as a forager might see the fields and streams: as holding undiscovered treasures to be sniffed out on foraging expeditions.

Here's one of my routes. I get on my motor scooter (other than my feet, my favorite conveyance for urban foraging) and head to Bryan's. This butcher is small and family-owned (two great characteristics of a foraging find) and it's been in business since 1963. They have the most incredible meats, poultry, fish, and prepared foods. I talk to the butcher about what I'm making that night and he or she will pick out the very best for me. I put everything in a satchel that I carry on my back, then head to my favorite neighborhood bakery, La Boulangerie, for bread and a chat with the owner, Pascal. Last, I go to Waxen Moon to look for candles for my table.

Asparagus Salad with Brown Butter and Meyer Lemons

My mother used to call our little Massachusetts town the asparagus capital of the world. Little did I know then that California had asparagus fields that stretched forever.

2 eggs

3 tablespoons unsalted butter

3 tablespoons extra-virgin olive oil

2 tablespoons Meyer lemon juice or regular lemon juice

1 tablespoon white wine vinegar

1 shallot, minced

Salt and freshly ground black pepper

1½ pounds fresh asparagus, ends removed

Place the eggs in a saucepan and cover with plenty of water. Bring to a boil and remove from the heat. Let sit in the water until completely cooked, 10 to 12 minutes. Peel and chop the eggs; reserve.

Place the butter in a small saucepan over medium-high heat. Cook the butter until it begins to foam and then the foam subsides. Continue to cook until the white solids turn to a rich golden brown and the butter just begins to smoke. Remove from the heat immediately.

In a small bowl, whisk together the butter, olive oil, lemon juice, white wine vinegar, and shallot. Season with salt and pepper.

Ten minutes before serving, bring a large saucepan of salted water to a boil. Add the asparagus and cook until tender, 5 to 7 minutes. Immediately place on a platter and drizzle with the vinaigrette. Sprinkle the reserved egg on top and serve immediately.

SERVES 6

WINE SUGGESTION: Dry sherry like fino, manzanilla, or amontillado

Farro, Pesto, and Tomato Salad

Inspiration for this recipe comes from my Tuscan friend and restaurateur, Giovanni Cappelli. Farro resembles reddish-brown rice and grows mainly in Tuscany and Umbria. Its crunchy texture and nutty flavor make it perfect for soups, stews, and salads. You'll find it in well-stocked food stores, Italian markets, or online at www.agferrari.com.

2 cups farro (about 8 ounces)

1/4 cup pine nuts, toasted

1 1/2 cups packed fresh basil leaves

1/2 cup freshly grated Parmigiano-Reggiano cheese

2 cloves garlic, minced

1/4 cup extra-virgin olive oil

Salt and freshly ground black pepper

3 medium tomatoes, cut into 1/2-inch dice

Basil leaves as a garnish

Place the farro in a large bowl and cover with plenty of cold water. Let sit for 2 hours.

Meanwhile, warm a small skillet over medium heat. Add the pine nuts and cook, stirring and shaking the pan constantly, until light golden, about 2 minutes. Remove from the pan immediately.

Place the basil, Parmigiano, and garlic in a blender or food processor and process until a coarse paste forms. Add the olive oil, salt and pepper to taste and process until the pesto is smooth.

Drain the farro. Place in a saucepan and with enough water to cover by at least 2 inches. Bring to a boil over high heat. Reduce the heat and simmer until the farro is tender but still crunchy, 10 to 20 minutes. Drain and let cool.

In a large bowl, toss together the farro and pesto and mix well. Add the pine nuts and tomatoes and stir together just until mixed. Season to taste with salt and pepper. Serve garnished with basil leaves.

SERVES 6

WINE SUGGESTION: Sauvignon Blanc or Vernaccia di San Girmignano

Farro Salad with Prosciutto and Grapefruit

One of the great things about city living is impromptu dinners. Call my brother; call a friend; they call a friend—and suddenly we have a dinner party. This often happens when I'm talking to my friend Kraemer. When I told her about this farro salad and she said, "Hmmm. Sounds like an interesting combination; I never would have thought of that," I knew by her tone that she wasn't sure, so I invited her for dinner and made this salad. She loved it. If you are having a tough time finding grapefruit or lemon oil, there is an American company called "O" that makes an amazing version, which is available at Sur La Table and other well-stocked gourmet markets.

> 1 cup farro (about 4 ounces)
> 3 grapefruit (pink, yellow, or a variety)
> 2 tablespoons grapefruit or lemon oil
> 1 tablespoon extra-virgin olive oil
> 3 tablespoons grapefruit juice
> 1 tablespoon white wine vinegar
> 2 teaspoons grapefruit zest
> Salt and freshly ground black pepper
> 1/2 English cucumber, halved, seeded, and cut into 1/4-inch dice
> 12 paper-thin slices prosciutto (about 4 ounces)
> Whole leaves of Italian parsley as a garnish

Place the farro in a bowl and cover with plenty of cold water. Let sit for 2 hours.

Meanwhile, using a sharp knife, cut the tops and bottoms off the grapefruit to reveal the colored flesh. Place one of the cut side downs down on a work surface. Using a small sharp knife, cut off the peel and white pith from top to bottom. Turn the fruit to the opposite cut side and remove any white pith. Cut the grapefruit into slices, removing the seeds. Place on a serving platter.

In a small bowl, whisk together the grapefruit oil and olive oil. Whisk in the grapefruit juice, vinegar, and grapefruit zest. Season with salt and pepper.

Drain the farro and place in a saucepan with enough cold water to cover by 2 inches. Bring to a boil, reduce the heat, and simmer until tender but crunchy, 10 to 20 minutes. Drain and let cool.

In a bowl, combine the farro, cucumber, and three-quarters of the vinaigrette. Season with salt and pepper. Pour the remaining vinaigrette onto the grapefruit slices.

To serve, top the grapefruit with the farro salad, spreading it out over the grapefruit. Place the prosciutto on top, twisting and turning it like ribbons. Garnish with the parsley.

SERVES 6

WINE SUGGESTION: Sauvignon Blanc

A BOWL OF FRUIT

I like to set out bowls of seasonal produce on my dining table, occasional table, and kitchen island. It makes a great edible decoration and also reminds us of the season. For example:

Spring: Cherries and strawberries
Summer: Plums, nectarines, apricots, peaches
Autumn: Pears, apples, quince
Winter: Pomegranates and satsuma tangerines; all kinds of
    citrus—lemons, oranges, limes

Thai Beef Salad with Mint and Cilantro

Sometimes I crave this salad. It's a breeze to make, especially if you have leftover grilled steak. (The next time you're grilling, put on an extra steak and then use it the next day for this salad.) If you don't particularly like hot, spicy food, temper the amount of serrano chile and cayenne you add. If you're like me and you do like hot food, boost the cayenne to your liking. In place of beef tenderloin, you could use fresh, cooked squid rings.

1 pound beef tenderloin, thinly
    sliced
1 serrano chile, seeded and minced
3 tablespoons fresh lime juice
2 tablespoons fish sauce or
    nam pla
2 teaspoons grated fresh ginger
1 teaspoon sugar
Large pinch of cayenne pepper
$\frac{1}{2}$ cup coarsely chopped fresh mint

$\frac{1}{3}$ cup thinly sliced red onion
$\frac{1}{2}$ English cucumber, unpeeled,
    halved, seeded, and thinly
    sliced
2 scallions, white and green parts,
    thinly sliced diagonally
Salt
8 small romaine leaves, cut
    crosswise into 1-inch strips
$\frac{1}{2}$ cup cilantro sprigs as garnish

Bring a pot of salted water to a boil. Place the beef in a small colander and dip the colander into the boiling water until the beef is cooked to medium rare, 20 to 30 seconds. Drain the beef.

In a large bowl, whisk together the serrano, lime juice, fish sauce, ginger, sugar, and cayenne. Add the beef, mint, onion, cucumber, and scallions and toss together. Season with salt.

To serve, place the lettuce on a large platter. Top with the beef salad and garnish with the cilantro.

SERVES 6

WINE SUGGESTION: Brouilly or Côtes du Rhône

Shrimp, Papaya, and Avocado Salad

In the dead of winter, when there's little or no fruit to be found in the market, I turn to papaya, which tastes of pure sunshine. I was inspired to make this salad after tasting a similar version in Mexico City. This makes an ideal luncheon salad or first course.

1¼ pounds large shrimp

1 medium papaya (about 1½ pounds)

2 avocados, peeled and sliced into ¼-inch slices (see Slicing an Avocado,
    page 106)

3 tablespoons extra-virgin olive oil

3 tablespoons chopped fresh cilantro

2 tablespoons fresh lime juice

Salt and freshly ground black pepper

¼ cup whole fresh cilantro leaves as a garnish

Lime wedges as a garnish

Place 2 cups of water in a frying pan and bring to a boil. Add the shrimp and simmer for 30 seconds. Remove from the heat and let the shrimp sit in the water for 30 minutes. Peel the shrimp and discard the shells. Reserve the shrimp in a bowl.

With a paring knife, peel the papaya. Cut in half and remove the seeds. Cut the papaya into slices and place the slices on a serving platter in a single layer. Place the avocado slices on top of the papaya overlapping.

In a small bowl, whisk together the olive oil, chopped cilantro, and lime juice. Season with salt and pepper. Combine half of the vinaigrette with the shrimp and place the shrimp on top of the papaya and avocado. Drizzle the remaining vinaigrette onto the papaya and avocado. Garnish with the cilantro leaves and lime wedges and serve.

SERVES 6

WINE SUGGESTION: Pinot Gris or Chardonnay

Shrimp Salad with White Beans, Mint Oil, and Watercress

This delicious, deceptively simple salad is a cinch to prepare after a long day.

1½ pounds jumbo shrimp, peeled

6½ tablespoons extra-virgin olive oil

Salt and freshly ground black pepper

30 fresh mint leaves

1 can cannellini beans (15 ounces), drained and rinsed

1 teaspoon lemon juice

1 large bunch watercress, tough stems removed

Mint sprigs as a garnish

Lemon wedges as a garnish

Preheat a broiler and set the oven rack 5 inches from the heat source.

Place the shrimp on a baking sheet, toss with 1 tablespoon of the olive oil, and spread them out in a single layer. Season with salt and pepper. Broil for 1½ minutes, turn, and broil 1½ minutes longer, until pink and slightly firm to the touch.

Bring a pot of water to a boil. Add the mint leaves and blanch for 20 seconds. Drain. Place the mint leaves in a blender or food processor and puree. With the motor running, slowly add 5 tablespoons of the olive oil to the mint and process for 30 seconds. Scrape down the sides and continue to puree until smooth, 30 to 60 seconds longer. In a bowl, toss the mint oil, shrimp, and cannellini beans together. Season with salt and pepper.

Whisk the remaining ½ tablespoon olive oil with the lemon juice. Season with salt and pepper. Toss with the watercress and place on a platter. Mound the white beans and shrimp on top of the watercress. Garnish with the mint sprigs and lemon wedges and serve immediately.

SERVES 6

WINE SUGGESTION: Chardonnay or rosé

Japanese Pickled Vegetable Salad

Anybody who knows me knows that I am as obsessed with dieting as I am with food. That's probably why I like Japanese food so much: it's low in calories but high in flavor, like Japanese pickled vegetables. Japanese markets carry a wide variety. In Japantown, just a few blocks from my house, my favorite market carries pickled carrots, daikon, cucumbers, and cabbage. One of the best uses for pickled vegetables is to add them to a salad of arugula and thinly shredded cabbage. I make the dressing with a small amount of oil, using the pickling juices in place of vinegar.

> 1/4 cup pickling juice
> 3 tablespoons vegetable oil
> 1 tablespoon rice vinegar
> 1 teaspoon finely grated fresh ginger
> Salt
> 6 cups arugula, stems removed
> 1 1/2 cups thinly sliced Savoy or napa cabbage
> 1 1/2 cups pickled vegetables (about 6 ounces), cut into thin julienne strips

Place the pickling juices, vegetable oil, vinegar, and ginger in a bowl and whisk together. Season with salt.

Place the arugula, cabbage, and pickled vegetables in a large bowl. Add the vinaigrette and toss together. Serve immediately.

SERVES 6

WINE SUGGESTION: Sake

Gravlax with Spring Salad

Gravlax is a Scandinavian dish prepared by burying salmon in salt, sugar, and dill. The name translates to "buried salmon," or *graved lax*. In Oslo, it is not uncommon to start the day with a large plate of gravlax and, for the heartiest of souls, to wash it down with a glass of aquavit. It's also a popular first course. I love it just by itself or, better yet, with this springtime salad. If there are leftovers, store them in the refrigerator tightly wrapped in plastic wrap for up to a week.

GRAVLAX

1¼ pounds center-cut salmon
   fillet, with skin intact, boned
½ cup chopped fresh dill
½ cup chopped fresh chives
2 tablespoons kosher salt
1½ tablespoons sugar
2 teaspoons crushed black
   peppercorns

SALAD

3 tablespoons extra-virgin olive oil
2 tablespoons champagne vinegar
   or white wine vinegar
2 teaspoons Dijon mustard
Salt and freshly ground black pepper
2 heads Belgian endive
1 large bunch watercress, stems
   removed
12 radishes, trimmed and tops
   removed, thinly sliced
1 small English cucumber, washed
   and unpeeled, thinly sliced

Prepare the gravlax: Cut salmon into 2 equal pieces. Place 1 piece of the salmon skin side down in a glass dish. In a small bowl, combine the dill, chives, salt, sugar, and crushed peppercorns. Spread the mixture on top of the fish. Top with the other piece of fish, skin side up. Cover the fish with plastic wrap and then with aluminum foil. Weight the fish with a flat 5-pound weight such as a brick. Refrigerate the salmon for 48 to 72 hours, turning and basting the fish with the accumulated juices in the dish every 24 hours.

Remove the salmon from the refrigerator, turn it flesh side up, and scrape off the herb mixture. With a sharp slicing knife, thinly slice the salmon on the diagonal. Place a layer of several slices of gravlax on the bottom of a platter.

Make the salad: In a small bowl, whisk together the olive oil, vinegar, and mustard. Season with salt and pepper.

Cut about 1 inch of the top off one piece of endive on a sharp diagonal. Turn the endive and continue to make diagonal cuts so that the pieces of endive are all about the same size. Repeat with the remaining endive.

Combine the endive with the watercress, radishes, and cucumbers. Toss with the vinaigrette to mix as well. Place the salad on top of the gravlax and serve.

SERVES 6

WINE SUGGESTION: Sparkling wine, champagne, or aquavit

"New York is so situated that anything you want, you can get in the very block you live in.... If you want pastrami or gefilte fish, there is a delicatessen every other door."

WILL ROGERS

Grilled Squid Salad with Winter Citrus

Sometimes when you're living in the city, an outdoor grill isn't easily accessible—especially in the winter. That's when I get out my cast-iron, nonstick, stainless or hard-anodized, indoor, ridged grill pan. I simply place the pan on the burner (mine is gas, but electric is fine here) and heat it over medium heat for ten minutes. I call it "convenience grilling." I love it because I can get away with using less oil and still get those great grill marks so distinctive of grilling. I swear by it—try it out!

1 grapefruit	1 tablespoon rice wine vinegar
2 navel oranges	Salt and freshly ground black
1/2 lemon	pepper
1/4 cup corn or peanut oil	1 small bunch frisée, ends removed
3 tablespoons fresh orange juice	3 scallions, white and green parts,
1 tablespoon freshly grated	thinly sliced diagonally
ginger	1 1/4 pounds fresh squid

Grate 1/4 teaspoon zest each from the grapefruit, oranges, and lemon and combine in a bowl. Add the 3 tablespoons of the corn oil, orange juice, ginger, and rice wine vinegar. Season with salt and pepper.

Meanwhile, heat an outdoor charcoal grill. Using a sharp knife, cut the tops and bottoms off the grapefruit to reveal the colored flesh. Place one of the cut sides down on a work surface. Using a small sharp knife, cut off the peel and white pith from top to bottom. Turn the fruit to the opposite cut side and remove any white pith. Cut the grapefruit into sections, cutting between the membrane. Discard any seeds. Repeat with the navel oranges and lemon. Place in a bowl with the frisée and scallions.

Separate the head and tentacles from the body of the squid. Cut the head from the tentacles and discard the head. Squeeze the top part of the tentacles inside out, to remove the beak. Set the tentacles aside in a colander.

Remove the clear quill bone from inside the body of each squid and discard. With a knife, scrape away the skin, cleaning out the inside of the body at the same time. Cut the squid from top to bottom to open the squid body completely. Cut the bottom $\frac{1}{2}$ inch off the squid body to make a rectangle. The rectangles shouldn't be much larger than 2 inches square. If so, cut them smaller. Score each square of the squid body with cross-hatched markings, being careful not to cut through the body completely. Add the bodies to the colander with the tentacles and wash well with cold water until the water runs clear. Dry on paper towels. Place in a bowl and toss with the remaining 1 tablespoon oil.

Place the pieces of squid on a hot grill or in a hot grill pan and cook until opaque, 45 to 60 seconds. Remove immediately and place in the bowl with the citrus and frisée. Toss well with the vinaigrette. Place on a platter and serve immediately.

SERVES 6

WINE SUGGESTION: Chardonnay

SQUID

There are really only two ways to cook squid well and to keep its tenderness: either very quickly over high heat (e.g., grilled, as in this recipe) or very slowly (e.g., braised for a long, long time). If you try for something in between, you'll have squid that is tough and chewy, like a piece of bubble gum you have chewed too long.

And remember that squid is one of the most perishable seafoods. Hopefully, you've bought it fresh. Keep it on a bed of ice until you're ready to cook it.

Duck Salad with Pecans and Kumquats

The last time I was at my favorite butcher picking up a few duck breasts, someone next to me asked how I cook duck. It's really easy; the only thing is that you must not over-cook it. If you remember this, everything else will be a breeze! This wonderful winter duck recipe calls for verjuice (literally "green juice"), traditionally made in France from unripe grapes but now available here at specialty gourmet shops. I use it because it is a wine-friendly alternative to vinegar. Kumquats are available in the winter. If you have difficulty locating them, substitute orange sections.

3 duck breast halves with skin (about 1½ pounds total)
Salt and freshly ground black pepper
½ cup pecans
3 tablespoons extra-virgin olive oil
½ teaspoon sugar
2 tablespoons verjuice, optional
1 tablespoon sherry vinegar
1 tablespoon hazelnut oil
10 to 12 cups assorted baby salad greens
12 kumquats, thinly sliced, seeds removed

Preheat the oven to 400°F. Place the duck breasts on a work surface, skin side up. Using a sharp knife, score the skin in a grid pattern, going through half of the thickness of the skin, but not through to the meat.

Heat a large skillet over medium-high heat. When the pan is hot, add the duck breasts, skin side down, and cook until the skin is golden and the fat from the skin has rendered. Turn the duck breasts, season with salt and pepper, place in the oven and cook until the duck breasts are medium rare, 6 to 8 minutes. Remove from the oven, cover with foil, and let rest for 10 minutes. Cut each duck breast on the diagonal into ¼-inch slices. Set aside.

Meanwhile, place the pecans on a baking sheet and drizzle with 1 tablespoon of the olive oil. Sprinkle with the sugar and salt. Bake until the pecans smell nutty and are very hot to the touch, 5 to 7 minutes. Remove from the oven and let cool.

In a small bowl, whisk together the verjuice, sherry vinegar, remaining 2 tablespoons of the olive oil, and the hazelnut oil. Season with salt and pepper.

In a large bowl, toss the greens, duck, pecans, and kumquats with the vinaigrette. Place on a platter and serve immediately.

SERVES 6

WINE SUGGESTION: Pinot Noir or Viognier

TWO FOR THE ROAD

Here are two of my favorite portable menus.

Ferry Boat to the Island Menu
Croutons with Tapenade, Orange, and Fennel (page 53)
Yellow Tomato Gazpacho (page 143)
Duck Salad with Pecans and Kumquats (page 138)
Little Almond and Plum Galettes (page 271)

Sailboat Menu
Farro, Pesto, and Tomato Salad (page 127)
Herb-Crusted Tuna Skewers with Tomato Aïoli (page 205)
Flakiest Apricot and Raspberry Tart (page 279)

At Home in the City

The neighborhood I live in is crossed by one of this city's busiest streets, a thorough-fare linking the downtown and outer residential neighborhoods. The buildings are tall and old, mostly Victorian-era beauties we endearingly call "Painted Ladies." Many of the buildings have street-level storefronts. Trees are in short supply. Speed, energy, and noise are not.

But when I close my front door, it is not so much to shut out the excitement and bustle as to be propelled by it. I love the energy of this city, of all cities. I love to know it's all out there at my fingertips. I try to keep my nerve endings as open to the city as possible. My office window overlooks the aforementioned busy street. Every other room in my house has at least one large window with a different view of the city, and I almost always keep them open to the air and sounds. I let that energy in through the food I cook, too, re-creating or adapting dishes I've had here or in other cities.

Of course, sometimes I need a little peace and serenity to renew myself. But how do I relax when all about me is this wild electricity? I remember that city living is also about slow food (away with fast food!). I remind myself to enjoy not just the eat-ing, but the whole celebration of food and dining, whether I'm by myself or with my family and friends. This seems especially important in the city where too often the pace of life hurries us to a grabbed snack on the run. So I try to take the time to make homemade stock, ice cream, and lots of soup. But I also try to be smart. I make extra of almost everything and freeze it.

With my crazy schedule—running from one place to another, planes, taxis, classes and meetings—I sometimes even miss a meal. So I try to make up in quality what I miss in quantity. On a foggy night (and there are a lot of these in San Francisco), soup and Tuscan bread grilled in my fireplace can calm the pace of life and make me glad that I am at home in the city.

Yellow Tomato Gazpacho

I have such a busy travel schedule that I love to make soups because when I'm home, they connect me to it in a really visceral way. Sometimes during the summer I will go to the farmers' market and buy a case of the best heirloom tomatoes, and then for the next few days I cook everything that I can think of using tomatoes. (Considering I wrote a whole book on tomatoes, *You Say Tomato*, with 250 tomato recipes, it isn't that surprising!) If yellow tomatoes are unavailable, by all means substitute red tomatoes.

SOUP

6 large ripe yellow tomatoes, peeled, seeded, and chopped
1 yellow bell pepper, seeded and coarsely chopped
1 yellow onion, coarsely chopped
1 large cucumber, peeled, halved, seeded, and coarsely chopped
6 tablespoons white wine vinegar
3 large cloves garlic, minced
3 tablespoons extra-virgin olive oil
1 slice stale Italian or French bread, crusts discarded, soaked in water and squeezed dry
Kosher salt and freshly ground black pepper

GARNISHES

2 tablespoons extra-virgin olive oil
3 cloves garlic, peeled and crushed
6 slices coarse-textured Italian or French bread, crusts discarded, torn into 3/4-inch pieces
1 1/2 cups red or colored cherry tomatoes (about 5 ounces), quartered
1/4 cup diced green bell pepper
1/4 cup peeled, seeded, and chopped cucumber
1/4 cup diced red onion

Make the soup: In a bowl, mix the tomatoes, bell pepper, onion, cucumber, vinegar, garlic, olive oil, and bread together. Using a blender, puree the mixture in batches, on high speed, until very smooth, 3 minutes. Strain through a coarse strainer. Season with kosher salt and black pepper. Refrigerate until well chilled.

Preheat the oven to 375°F.

Prepare the garnish: Warm the olive oil in a small saucepan over medium- high heat. Add the crushed garlic and cook, stirring occasionally, until the garlic is light golden, 1 minute. Discard the garlic. Place the bread in a single layer on a baking sheet. Drizzle the garlic oil and salt over the bread and toss together. Bake, tossing the bread cubes occasionally, until golden, 10 to 12 minutes.

To serve, ladle the chilled soup into bowls and garnish with the croutons, tomatoes, green peppers, cucumber, and red onion. Serve immediately.

SERVES 6

WINE SUGGESTION: Rosé or a dry sherry like fino, manzanilla, or amontillado

YOU SAY TOMATO

My grandmother used to grow all different shapes, sizes, and colors of tomatoes in her garden. I didn't make much of it until I began working at Chez Panisse, when I realized that my grandmother had in fact been growing heirloom tomatoes, which had now become incredibly fashionable. (Well, I did always think my grandmother was pretty cool . . .)

The dictionary defines heirloom as "a valued possession passed down in a family through succeeding generations." This wonderful term applies not just to heirloom tomatoes, but also to heirloom apples, peaches, and many vegetables.

Countless original tomato varieties were lost fifty to one hundred years ago, and hybrid tomatoes, like Early Girl, Better Boy, and Big Boy, took over. Heirloom tomatoes don't ship as well, don't keep as long, and are less disease-resistant, but they have better, more intense flavor and tenderness.

HEIRLOOM TOMATOES, A TO Z

Ace; Azoychka; Brandywine; Caro Rich; Cherokee Purple; Costoluto Genovese; Dad's Mug; Dorothy's Green; Eva Purple Ball; Goldie; Green Grape; Green Zebra; Marvel Striped; Old German; Orange Cherry; Palestinina; Pineapple Tomato; Principe Borghese Italian Drying; Pruden's Purple; Red Currant; Southern Night; Stupice; Super Italian Paste; White Queen; Yellow Bell; Yellow Pear; Zebra

Champagne Oyster Soup
with Celery and Fennel

Oysters. You either love them or hate them. I happen to love them and began eating them when I was very young (although this was more to please my father, who loved them, too). This soup is perfect for a special celebration served with a glass of icy cold champagne.

2 dozen fresh oysters in their shell

2 tablespoons butter

3 bulbs fennel, cut into ½-inch dice, tops chopped and reserved for garnish

5 stalks celery, cut into ½-inch slices

2 onions, cut into ½-inch dice

1 pound potatoes, peeled and cut into ½-inch cubes

2 cups water

2 cups bottled clam juice or fish stock

1 cup champagne or sparkling wine

½ cup heavy cream

Salt and freshly ground black pepper

Celery leaves as a garnish

Shuck the oysters with their oyster liquor and refrigerate. Discard the shells.

Melt the butter in a soup pot over medium-low heat. Add the fennel, celery, and onions and cook until the vegetables begin to soften, 15 minutes. Add the potatoes, water, clam juice, and champagne and simmer until the potatoes are tender, about 15 minutes.

Remove one-quarter of the soup and puree in a blender on high speed until very smooth, about 3 minutes. Strain in a fine-mesh strainer and add the pureed mixture back into the soup base. Stir in the cream and season to taste with salt and pepper.

Just before serving, heat the soup, stirring occasionally, until very hot over medium heat. Add the oysters and their liquor and simmer for 1 minute. Ladle the soup into bowls and garnish with chopped celery leaves and fennel tops.

SERVES 6

WINE SUGGESTION: Chardonnay or champagne

Miso Soup with Edamame

I am so lucky that just a hot-skip-and-a-jump from my house is San Francisco's Japan-town, an urban village of noodle shops, sushi bars, and antique and gift shops. The best part is that I have a love affair with Japanese food. I often walk down for a bowl of noo-dles or a few pieces of sushi accompanied by edamame, the bright green soy beans that are good for you and equally delicious. And it always seems that I am served a bowl of miso soup to begin my meal. I love to eat this soup anytime and have learned to make it at home. It's not only easy to make, it's infinitely more delicious made fresh like this. By the way, wakame is a type of seaweed; dashi is a stock made from bonito flakes; and shiro miso is white fermented-soybean paste. You can find these ingredients in Asian markets, health food, or natural food markets.

> $1/4$ cup dried wakame
> $1/4$ cup shiro miso
> 6 cups dashi (recipe follows)
> $1/2$ pound soft tofu, drained and cut into $1/2$-inch cubes
> $1/2$ cup peeled edamame
> $1/4$ cup thinly sliced scallions

Place the wakame in a bowl with enough water to cover by 1 inch. Let stand for 15 minutes. Drain through a fine-mesh strainer. Chop coarsely.

Place the miso and $1/4$ cup of the dashi in a bowl and stir together until smooth.

Heat the remaining $5^3/4$ cups dashi in a large saucepan over medium-high heat until hot. Stir in the tofu gently and the drained wakame. Add the edamame and simmer for 1 minute. Remove from the heat and immediately add the miso and scal-lions. Stir well and serve immediately.

SERVES 6

WINE SUGGESTION: Sake

Dashi

6 cups cold water

1 ounce (30 grams) kombu (dried kelp), about 20 square inches

2 (5-gram) packages katsuo bushi (dried bonito flakes), about 1 cup

Bring the cold water and kombu just to a boil in a large saucepan over high heat. Remove from the heat and discard the kombu. Sprinkle the katsuo bushi over the liquid and let stand for 3 minutes. If necessary, stir to make the katsuo bushi sink. Pour through a cheesecloth-lined sieve or a coffee filter into a bowl.

MAKES 6 CUPS

> *"I have never felt salvation in nature. I love cities above all."*
>
> MICHELANGELO

Gratin of Tomato and Eggplant Soup

I was recently in Provence, France, looking for new locations for my courses. Staying in the lovely hilltop village of Gordes, I frequented the market. One day I found the best tomatoes and eggplant. Here is what I came up with. Enjoy!

> 1 medium eggplant (about 1 pound)
> Salt
> 3 tablespoons extra-virgin olive oil
> 8 plum tomatoes (about 1½ pounds)
> 3 cloves garlic, 1 whole and 2 minced
> ¼ cup chopped parsley
> Freshly ground black pepper
> 5 cups homemade chicken stock, heated
> 1 cup finely grated Parmigiano-Reggiano cheese

Preheat the oven to 400°F. Cut the eggplant into ⅓-inch slices. Salt lightly on both sides and place on paper towels in a single layer. Let stand for 30 minutes. Wash well and dry completely with clean paper towels. Brush heavily with olive oil and place on a baking sheet. Bake, turning occasionally until golden on each side, 15 to 20 minutes. Cut the slices in half.

Bring a large pot of water to a boil. Add the tomatoes and boil for 30 seconds. Place in a bowl of ice water. Core the tomatoes and slice into ⅜-inch slices.

Stir together the minced garlic and the parsley. Reserve.

Rub a 2-quart gratin dish with the remaining whole clove of garlic. Oil the gratin dish. Place a single row of tomatoes at one end of the gratin dish. Overlap with a row of eggplant on top of the tomatoes. Sprinkle lightly with the garlic-parsley mixture and season with salt and pepper. Repeat until the gratin dish is filled and you have used all of the eggplant and tomatoes and all except 1 tablespoon of the garlic-parsley mixture. Ladle 1 cup of the hot chicken stock into the gratin dish. Sprinkle

with $^3/_4$ cup of the cheese. Bake in the oven until the liquid is almost absorbed, about 45 minutes.

Season the hot chicken stock with salt and pepper. Spoon a large scoop of the gratin into each soup bowl. Ladle the stock into the bowls. Garnish with the remaining garlic-parsley mixture and the remaining $^1/_4$ cup cheese and serve immediately.

SERVES 6

WINE SUGGESTION: Sauvignon Blanc, Sangiovese, or Côtes du Rhône

WHY YOU HAVE TO MAKE
HOMEMADE CHICKEN STOCK

There are certain dishes that you just can't make well without homemade stock. Pasta in Brodo, the Italian soup that is basically pasta in broth, depends on good stock. So do risotto and sauces. (Canned stocks don't have as much flavor and have too high a concentration of salt.) I consider good stock such an essential ingredient that I always have it on hand in my freezer. I mean, culinarily speaking, I would feel naked if I didn't. So when I make it, I make a ton (maybe not a ton, but at least gallons). Besides, it's really easy to make.

This is my basic recipe. It makes a good-quality stock with lots of flavor:

1. For each 5 pounds of chicken bones (backs, necks, and breast bones), add 1 onion, 1 carrot, 3 sprigs of parsley, a pinch of fresh or dried thyme, and 1 bay leaf.
2. Put everything in a stockpot and add enough water to cover the bones by 1 to 2 inches, even if the stockpot goes up to the ceiling and you have only 2 inches of bones.

3. Bring everything to a boil, then immediately reduce the heat to low and let simmer (I like to say simmer, but I really mean shiver or tremble). Cook, uncovered, for 5 to 6 hours. The only thing I do during this time is to replenish the liquid to the original level as it cooks down.

4. Strain the stock; discard the bones and vegetables; place the stock in a bowl and put it in the refrigerator until cool (preferably overnight). The next day, skim off all the fat, put the stock in plastic containers, and freeze for up to 1 month.

When I'm making chicken stock, I like to use the back, neck, and breastbones of the chicken (which I get from my butcher) rather than chicken parts with meat on them. This is because the flavor in stock comes from where the meat attaches to the bone and not from the meat itself. You can use wings, but they produce a lot of fat because of the skin. Some Chinese cooks use chicken feet, but that produces a really gelatinous stock. So I like to use the bones.

I don't like to add celery to stock, because it's quite strong in flavor. But if I did, I'd just add a one-inch piece. If I happened to have leeks in the house, I'd add one; but, honestly, I never have extra on hand, so I don't. I might add a few peppercorns for flavor, but I usually forget them. I try to keep it simple.

Hot and Sour Soup

When I first started to shop in Chinatown, I felt so foreign. I remember looking at every package, smelling every spice. Now it's second nature and I really love my trips to Chinatown. I have my favorite place for vegetables, fish, and staples. And in San Francisco, we have such a big Chinese population that we have three Chinatowns. I make this soup when I need a boost! Serve it with cold beer or hot tea.

2 whole wood ear mushrooms or
    1/2 cup slivered wood ear
    mushrooms
3 dried black or shiitake
    mushrooms
5 cups chicken stock
6 ounces soft tofu, drained and
    diced
4 ounces bamboo shoots (about
    3/4 cup)
4 ounces lean boneless pork,
    thinly sliced
1 tablespoon minced fresh ginger
1 stalk lemon grass, bottom
    6 inches only, crushed

1/3 cup rice vinegar
3 tablespoons dark soy sauce
1/8 teaspoon cayenne pepper, or to
    taste
1 teaspoon sesame oil
1/2 teaspoon sugar
3 tablespoons cornstarch dissolved
    in 1/4 cup water
1 egg, lightly beaten
Chopped cilantro as a garnish
3 scallions, white and green parts,
    thinly sliced diagonally

Soak the wood ear mushrooms and black mushrooms in warm water to cover until softened, 30 minutes. Swish the mushrooms to dislodge any grit or dirt. Drain and slice them into thin slivers.

In a large soup pot, bring the stock to a boil over medium-high heat. Add the mushrooms, tofu, bamboo shoots, pork, ginger, and lemon grass. Reduce the heat to low and simmer, stirring occasionally, for 3 minutes. Add the vinegar, soy sauce, cayenne, sesame oil, and sugar. Simmer 3 minutes longer. Increase the heat to medium-high, add the cornstarch mixture, and cook, stirring, until the soup boils and thickens slightly.

Remove the lemon grass and discard. Remove the soup from the heat and slowly drizzle the egg, stirring in one direction, until the egg forms short threads. Ladle into bowls, garnish with cilantro and scallions, and serve immediately.

SERVES 6

> "The city has always been the fireplace of civilization, whence
>
> light and heat radiated out into the dark."
>
> THEODORE PARKER

Lobster, Roasted Pepper, Tomato, and Corn Chowder

A couple of months ago, I spent the weekend in Seattle with my dear friends, Renee and Carl Behnke, the owners of Sur La Table. My services had been auctioned off to create and cook a dinner for twelve at a lovely home on Puget Sound owned by friends of the Behnkes. Inspired by growing up in New England and eating Maine lobsters during my entire childhood, I created this chowder for their special dinner. It gave me great satisfaction when I heard their spoons cleaning the bottoms of their bowls. This soup requires some effort, but it is one of those times that it is really worth it.

2 live Maine lobsters (1¼ pounds each)

1 cup dry white wine (such as Sauvignon Blanc)

½ pound potatoes, peeled and diced

2 yellow or red bell peppers, roasted

6 small ears of fresh corn

2 tablespoons butter

1 yellow onion, chopped

1 pound yellow or red tomatoes, peeled, seeded, and chopped

½ cup heavy cream

Salt and freshly ground black pepper

2 tablespoons snipped chives as a garnish

Bring a large stockpot of water to a boil. Add the lobsters and cook for 10 minutes. Remove the lobsters and set aside to cool. Reserve the lobster broth. Cut the lobster in half from top to bottom and remove the meat from the lobster tail, dice, and set aside. Remove the meat from the claws, dice, and set aside with the tail meat. Discard the tomalley, gill tissues, and digestive tract. Cut the head section into small pieces. Reserve shells. In a saucepan, combine the shells, the wine, and 6 cups of the reserved lobster broth and bring to a boil. Reduce the heat to low and simmer for 20 minutes. Strain through a fine-mesh strainer and reserve.

In a large saucepan simmer the potatoes in salted water until tender, about 10 minutes. Drain.

Place the bell peppers directly over a gas flame and turn occasionally until black on all sides. Alternatively, cut the bell peppers in half lengthwise and remove the stems, seeds, and ribs; place cut side down on a baking sheet; and broil until the skin is blackened, about 10 minutes. Transfer the peppers to a plastic bag, close tightly, and let cool for 10 minutes. Remove the skin by scraping with a knife. Cut the peppers into 1-inch-wide strips and place in a bowl.

Shuck the corn and remove the kernels from the cob.

Melt the butter in a soup pot over medium-low heat. Add the onion and cook, stirring occasionally, until soft, about 10 minutes. Add half of the corn kernels, the roasted peppers, the tomatoes and the lobster broth and simmer for 20 minutes. Puree in a blender at high speed until very smooth. Strain through a fine sieve into a clean pan. Add the cream, lobster meat, reserved corn kernels, and the potatoes. Season with salt and pepper. Simmer until hot and the corn is tender, 3 to 4 minutes. Serve immediately, garnished with chives.

SERVES 6

WINE SUGGESTION: Sauvignon Blanc or Chardonnay

Yellow Split Pea and Carrot Soup with Cilantro Yogurt

OK, what was it that Mark Twain said? "The coldest winter I ever spent was a summer in San Francisco." Boy, was he right. So even in the summer (when we are socked in with fog), I make soups of all kinds. And when I do, I make a big pot so I have leftovers. What to do with them? Simple; I just put the extra soup in plastic containers and pop them in the freezer. That way, I have an instant and delicious meal, whether it's for lunch on a day I'm working at home or an impromptu late-night supper with my friends.

1½ cups yellow or orange split peas (about 10 ounces)
1 tablespoon olive oil
3 medium carrots, peeled and coarsely chopped
1 medium yellow onion, coarsely chopped
1½ teaspoons coarsely ground coriander seeds
8 cups chicken stock, vegetable stock, or water
Salt and freshly ground black pepper
½ cup yogurt
⅓ cup chopped cilantro

Pick over the split peas and discard any stones or damaged peas. Rinse the peas and drain.

Warm the olive oil in a soup pot over medium heat. Add the carrots, onion, and coriander seeds and cook, stirring occasionally, until the vegetables are soft, about 10 minutes. Add the stock and split peas, bring to a boil, reduce the heat, and simmer gently until the split peas are completely soft, 30 to 40 minutes.

Remove the soup from the heat. Let cool for 30 minutes. Working in small batches, puree the soup in a blender on high speed until smooth, about 2 minutes per batch. Thin with water or stock if the soup is too thick. Return the soup to a clean pan. Season with salt and pepper. Reheat the soup gently. Meanwhile, place the yogurt and cilantro in a bowl. Stir together. Season with salt and pepper.

To serve, ladle the soup into bowls, drizzle with the yogurt mixture and serve immediately.

SERVES 6

WINE SUGGESTION: Sauvignon Blanc, Pinot Gris, or Pinot Grigio

---

BABY, IT'S COLD OUTSIDE

Roasted Beet, Avocado, and Watercress Salad (page 105)

Yellow Split Pea and Carrot Soup with Cilantro Yogurt
   (page 158)

Cranberry Upside-Down Cake (page 283)

Kale Soup with Pancetta and White Beans

Bean soups like this one cross all economic lines in Italy and are eaten at every table, whether in the villas of the Tuscan nobility or the humble homes of the Sardinian peasant. When it's cold outside, this type of stick-to-your-ribs soup is eaten piping hot. But when it's hot outside, believe it or not, this soup is eaten chilled. Either way, a bowl of bean soup can be a satisfying meal in itself, in the country or the city.

2 cups cannellini beans (about
   1 pound)
2 tablespoons olive oil
1 yellow onion, minced
2 ounces pancetta, diced
8 cloves garlic, minced
12 cups chicken stock, vegetable stock, or water
3 cups kale, stems discarded, chopped
1 cup peeled, seeded, and chopped tomatoes (fresh or canned)
Salt and freshly ground black pepper
2 tablespoons extra-virgin olive oil

Pick over the beans and discard any stones or damaged beans. Cover with water and soak for 4 hours or overnight.

Heat the olive oil in a large soup pot over medium heat. Add the onion and pancetta and cook, stirring occasionally, until the pancetta starts to turn golden and the onion is soft, 10 to 12 minutes. Add the garlic and continue to cook, stirring, for 2 minutes. Add the beans and stock and bring to a boil. Reduce the heat to low and simmer gently for 1 to 1½ hours.

When the beans are tender, remove from the heat and let cool slightly. Puree one-quarter of the beans in a food processor or blender. Return the pureed beans to the soup. Add the kale and tomatoes and simmer the soup until the kale is tender, about 15 minutes. Season with salt and pepper.

Ladle the soup into bowls, drizzle with the extra virgin olive oil and serve immediately.

SERVES 6

WINE SUGGESTION: Chianti or Beaujolais

> "It is impossible to reminisce about San Francisco without thinking of food. As an international overeater I would not hesitate to take any European gourmet and invite him to lean his paunch against the tables set by the restaurants there."
>
> PAUL GALLICO

Summer Tomato Soup with Basil Cream

OK, what constitutes a perfect marriage? Maybe when it comes to people that takes a lifetime to figure out. But with vegetables, it may very well be that tomatoes and basil are a perfect union. It's something about the sweetness in each that really brings out their best. For an even sweeter soup, peel, seed, and chop the tomatoes since tomato seeds tend to be bitter. The soup may be pureed in the blender or passed through a food mill fitted with the finest blade. It can be made up to one day in advance and stored in the refrigerator until ready to serve.

1 cup heavy cream
4 fresh basil sprigs
1 tablespoon olive oil
1 medium yellow onion, chopped
8 large ripe tomatoes (about 5 pounds), cored and quartered
4 cups chicken stock
1 cup water
Salt and freshly ground black pepper
$1/4$ cup finely chopped basil leaves as a garnish

Place the cream in a saucepan over medium-high heat until scalded. Add the coarsely chopped basil sprigs, turn off the heat, and let sit for 1 hour.

Heat the olive oil in a large soup pot over medium-high heat. Add the onion and cook, stirring occasionally, until soft, about 7 minutes. With kitchen string, tie the basil sprigs together. Add the tomatoes, chicken stock, and water and bring to a boil. Reduce the heat to low and simmer until reduced by one-quarter, about 20 minutes. Let cool for 10 minutes. Remove the basil sprigs.

In a blender, puree the soup in several batches on high speed until smooth, 2 to 3 minutes per batch. Strain into a clean soup pot and bring to a simmer over medium heat. Season with salt and pepper.

Strain the cream and discard the basil. Place the cream in a bowl and chill well. Whip the cream until soft peaks just begin to form. Add the finely chopped basil leaves. Season with salt and pepper.

To serve, heat the soup over medium heat until hot, 5 minutes. Ladle the soup into bowls and drizzle with cream. Serve immediately.

SERVES 6

WINE SUGGESTION: Chardonnay or Sangiovese

PEEL, CORE, SEED

PEELING: Bring a large saucepan of water to a boil. With a small, sharp knife, cut an X in the bottom of each tomato. Drop the tomatoes into the boiling water and boil for 15 to 20 seconds. Remove with tongs or a slotted spoon. Let sit until cool enough to handle, then peel off the skins. Forget the ice water bath sometimes recommended after boiling or blanching tomatoes—it just dilutes the flavor.

Alternatively, tomatoes can be peeled with a very sharp serrated vegetable peeler, sawing with a back-and-forth motion.

CORING: Using a small knife, cut a V-shaped indentation all around the core and lift it out.

SEEDING: You can seed fresh or canned tomatoes using the same easy method. Making believe the core is the North Pole, cut the tomato across the equator. Next, cup each tomato half in the palm of your hand, cut side exposed, and squeeze the seeds into a bowl. Discard the seeds.

Tortilla and Tomato Soup

All I need to make tortilla soup (the Mexican equivalent of "Jewish penicillin") is home-made chicken stock, a few pieces of chicken, seasonal vegetables, diced avocado, a lime, some grated cheese, and tortillas. If you don't want to go through the hassle of frying tortillas, buy crispy tortilla chips. This soup is more like a stew and is a meal in itself. If you want to get fancy, make a batch of hot cornbread to serve alongside.

2 tablespoons vegetable oil	2 bay leaves
2 large yellow onions, quartered, and thinly sliced	2 to 3 tablespoons fresh lime juice
5 cloves garlic, minced	Salt and freshly ground black pepper
1 whole chicken (3½ pounds), cut into 6 pieces, skin removed	Corn oil for frying the tortillas
8 cups water	5 corn tortillas, cut into ¼-inch strips
3 large tomatoes, peeled, seeded, and chopped	2 ounces mozzarella cheese, coarsely grated
3 teaspoons ground cumin	2 ounces Monterey Jack cheese, coarsely grated
2 teaspoons chili powder	1 large avocado, diced
½ teaspoon chopped fresh oregano	¼ cup sour cream

Heat the oil in a large soup pot over medium heat. Add the onions and cook until soft, about 7 minutes. Add the garlic and cook, stirring, for 1 minute. Add the chicken, water, tomatoes, cumin, chili powder, oregano, and bay leaves. Bring to a boil, reduce heat to low and simmer, uncovered, until the chicken is very tender, about 1 hour. Discard the bay leaves. You should have approximately 6 to 7 cups broth remaining. Remove the chicken from the pan. Remove the meat from the bones and discard the bones. Dice and return the chicken to the pot. Season to taste with the lime juice, salt and pepper.

Heat ¹/₂ inch corn oil in a deep heavy pan to 375°F on a deep-fat thermometer. Add the tortilla strips and cook until crispy, 1 minute. Remove from the pan and drain on paper towels.

To serve, heat the soup until hot. Ladle into bowls and garnish with the mozzarella, Monterey Jack, and avocado. Top with a spoonful of sour cream and the tortillas strips.

SERVES 6

WINE SUGGESTION: Sauvignon Blanc or Semillon

Tomato Rice Soup with Tiny Meatballs

I manage to visit Rome at least once a year. Call me a lucky girl, but when I go I like to visit one of my favorite restaurants, Piperno, in the Jewish Quarter. I usually sit outside, but one particular October evening we sat inside it was so chilly. As a further fortification against the cold, I ordered a bowl of this most comforting soup full of tomatoes, rice, and a few moist, spicy meatballs. Serve it as I had it that night with a glass of Chianti and some bruschetta (grilled bread rubbed with garlic and brushed with fruity extra-virgin olive oil). You can substitute ground beef, pork, or any combination in place of the veal.

3/4 pound ground veal

3/4 cup dry bread crumbs

2 cloves garlic, minced

1 tablespoon chopped fresh flat-leaf parsley

1 teaspoon ground coriander

1/4 teaspoon ground nutmeg

1/4 teaspoon ground cumin

Pinch of cayenne pepper

Salt and freshly ground black pepper

1 tablespoon olive oil

1 large yellow onion, coarsely chopped

1 carrot, coarsely chopped

1/2 stalk celery, coarsely chopped

5 cups chicken stock

2 cups water

5 large ripe red tomatoes, peeled, seeded, and chopped (fresh or canned)

1/2 cup long-grain white rice

Preheat an oven to 350°F. In a bowl, combine the veal, bread crumbs, garlic, parsley, coriander, nutmeg, cumin, cayenne, 1/2 teaspoon salt, and 1/8 teaspoon pepper. Form into 25 to 30 3/4-inch meatballs and place on a baking sheet. Bake for 10 to 12 minutes. Remove from oven and reserve.

Heat the olive oil in a large skillet over medium-low heat. Add the onion, carrot, and celery and cook, stirring occasionally, until soft, about 10 minutes. Add the chicken stock, water, and tomatoes. Cover and simmer until the tomatoes fall apart, 20 minutes. Let cool for 10 minutes.

In batches, puree the soup in a blender on high speed until very smooth, 3 minutes per batch. Place in a clean soup pot. Bring the soup to a simmer over medium heat. Add the rice, cover, and cook until almost tender, 10 minutes. Season to taste with salt and pepper. Add the meatballs and continue to cook until the rice is tender and the meatballs are hot, 5 minutes.

Ladle the soup into bowls and serve immediately.

SERVES 6

WINE SUGGESTION: Merlot, Chianti, or Cabernet

"O Rome! my country!

City of the soul!"

LORD BYRON

City Food

If you composed a soundtrack to city food, it would surely have to be a rhapsody of classical, jazz, rap, R&B, soul, pop, and ethnic music. For city food is nothing if not astonishingly eclectic in its inclusion of every culinary note. It has the loud notes of strong and direct flavors, bold, assertive colors, and the softer cadence of complex textures and unique ingredients. But it isn't just that. City food hums with a kind of energy all its own.

To live, cook, and eat in a modern city is to have access to an almost infinite variety of choice and diversity. There cannot ever have been a more amazing time to be a cook. I am constantly inspired to try new things, to cook with greater passion and more daring. I find I want to talk to the Chinatown chefs and then go home and apply their ideas in my own kitchen. I want to cook something audacious at a beach barbecue or do an incredible picnic on a sailboat. I want to open myself up to new tastes and experiences by experimenting with really exotic dishes and ingredients. I want to learn how the Thai cooks assemble such interesting flavors, and I want to make them myself and share them with my friends and family.

I love trying all of the newest or trendiest techniques and products, from poaching salmon in fruity olive oil to cooking it on a cedar plank, from making pizza out of phyllo dough to making grilled sandwiches on a panini maker. But I also love to do all that old-time stuff, too: braising and brining, hand-churning ice cream, and making upside-down cakes.

Maybe city food is just what we make of it, whether it's the fare at a greasy spoon, an all-night diner, a hole-in-the-wall neighborhood ethnic restaurant, or a sophisticated 3-star, white-tablecloth restaurant. It runs the gamut from a simple dinner of soup by the fire to an elaborate dinner by candlelight; from a homemade dish that is as good as anything you'd get in the finest restaurant to the simplest meal with your kids, to something your mother made with you when you were a child.

Maybe it's a cliché, but it seems like we really can have it all. That range of possibility is so incredibly interesting to me and may be at the heart of why I love to be in the city, cooking and eating city food.

Pan-Seared Chicken Breasts with Mustard, Rosemary, and Capers

This is one of my old standbys, meaning I keep the ingredients on standby so that I can make it when I need a quick but impressive dish. One of the reasons this recipe is so reliably good is that I brine the chicken first; soaking the chicken in a solution of water, vinegar, and salt yields the juiciest, most succulent chicken ever. If you like, you can substitute pork chops for the chicken and, if you are really pressed for time, you can omit the brining step. It will still be wonderful, just not quite as juicy and moist.

12 cups water

1 tablespoon white wine vinegar

3/4 cup kosher salt, plus more for seasoning

1 tablespoon olive oil

6 chicken breast halves, skin and bone attached (about 8 ounces each)

Freshly ground black pepper

2 cups chicken stock

1/3 cup capers

1 1/2 tablespoons mustard

1/2 teaspoon chopped fresh rosemary

Place the water and vinegar in a large bowl. Add the salt and stir together to dissolve. Add the chicken breasts and refrigerate for 3 hours. Remove the chicken from the water and dry well with paper towels.

Preheat the oven to 425°F. Heat the olive oil in a large ovenproof skillet over medium heat. Add the chicken breasts, skin side down, and cook until light golden, 5 to 6 minutes. Turn the chicken, season with salt and pepper, and cook until golden on the other side, 5 to 6 minutes. Place the pan in the oven and cook until the skin of the chicken is golden and the meat is cooked, 10 to 15 minutes. Transfer the chicken to a warm platter, cover with foil, and keep warm.

Pour off any excess fat from the pan. Place the pan back on high heat (be careful, the handle is very hot after being in the oven). Add the chicken stock and bring to a boil. Add the capers, mustard, and rosemary and simmer until the stock is reduced by half, about 5 minutes.

To serve, place one chicken breast on each plate and spoon the sauce over the chicken breasts.

SERVES 6

WINE SUGGESTION: Chardonnay or Pinot Noir

> *"Men come together in cities in order to live: they remain together in order to live the good life."*
>
> ARISTOTLE

Spice-Crusted Chicken Breasts with Cucumber Lemon Raita

Every year I have what I call an "office party." That is, I invite all of my friends without a "real" office (because they are other writers, artists, and chefs) to come to my house for a holiday party. One year, an "officeless" friend and I had been really intrigued with Indian food, so we decided to make that the theme. Here is a modern adaptation of an Indian dish that was created that night. Absolutely delicious!

2 cardamom pods

3 tablespoons coriander seeds

3 tablespoons cumin seeds

3 tablespoons fennel seeds

Salt and freshly ground black pepper

6 boneless chicken breast halves, with skin (6 ounces each)

2 tablespoons extra-virgin olive oil

½ English cucumber, unpeeled and grated

1¼ cups plain yogurt

1 tablespoon grated lemon zest

1 clove garlic, minced

⅛ teaspoon cayenne pepper

Lemon wedges as a garnish

Place the cardamom pods, coriander seeds, cumin seeds, fennel seeds, 1 teaspoon salt, and ½ teaspoon black pepper in an electric spice or coffee grinder and pulse until finely ground. Reserve 1 teaspoon. Place the remaining spice mixture on a plate. Brush the chicken breasts evenly with 1 tablespoon of the olive oil. Press the chicken breasts into the spice mixture, coating each side evenly.

Place the grated cucumber on several layers of paper towels and top with more paper towels. Pat well to remove the excess water from the cucumber. In a bowl, stir together the cucumber, yogurt, lemon zest, garlic, cayenne, and the reserved 1 teaspoon spice mixture. Season with salt and pepper. Reserve.

Warm the remaining 1 tablespoon olive oil in a large skillet over medium-high heat. Add the chicken breasts, skin side down, and cook in a single layer until the skin is golden, 3 to 5 minutes. Reduce the heat to low, turn the chicken breasts, season with salt and pepper and cook until done, 4 to 5 minutes longer.

Place 1 chicken breast on each plate, spoon the sauce alongside, garnish with lemon wedges, and serve immediately.

SERVES 6

WINE SUGGESTION: Sauvignon Blanc or Côtes du Rhône

> *"The crowd, and buzz and murmuring,*
>
> *Of this great hive, the city."*
>
> ABRAHAM COWLEY

Braised Chicken with Green Garlic

Green garlic is immature garlic harvested before the individual cloves are formed and encased with papery skin. It resembles a small leek or scallion, and the flavor is much milder and sweeter than mature garlic. If green garlic is unavailable, substitute 2 bulbs of regular mature garlic. Serve with Oven-Fried Potato Chips with Marjoram Salt (page 178) and plenty of crusty bread to mop up the irresistible sauce.

> 1 large chicken (about 4 pounds)
> 2 tablespoons unsalted butter
> 2 tablespoons extra-virgin olive oil
> Salt and freshly ground black pepper
> 1 cup water
> 3 heads green garlic bulbs, chopped (about 3/4 cup)
> 1 1/4 cups dry white wine (such as Sauvignon Blanc)
> 1 1/2 cups chicken stock

Remove the wings from the chicken and discard. Cut the chicken into 8 pieces, each breast half cut crosswise into 2 pieces, 2 thighs, and 2 drumsticks.

Melt the butter in the olive oil in a large skillet over medium-high heat. Working in batches if necessary, add the chicken, season with salt and pepper, and cook until golden brown on one side, 6 to 8 minutes. Turn the chicken pieces and cook until golden brown on the second side, another 6 to 8 minutes. Transfer the chicken to a platter; cover with foil, and keep warm. Pour the excess fat from the pan and discard.

Reduce the heat to medium, add the water and garlic, and cook until the garlic is soft and the water has almost evaporated, about 10 minutes. Add more water during cooking if necessary. Puree in a blender on high speed until very smooth; reserve.

Return the chicken to the pan and increase the heat to high. Add the white wine, chicken stock, and garlic paste and bring to a boil. Reduce the heat to low, cover, and simmer until the chicken can be easily skewered, 20 to 25 minutes. Season with salt and pepper.

Transfer the chicken to a platter and cover with foil. Over high heat, reduce the sauce until slightly thickened. Pour the sauce over the chicken and serve.

SERVES 6

WINE SUGGESTION: The same wine you made the braised chicken with, Sauvignon Blanc or Chardonnay

Oven-Fried Potato Chips with Marjoram Salt

I have to tell you a little secret: Potato chips are one of my weaknesses. If I eat one, I can't stop until I eat the whole bag. My family has to hide them from me. So I must warn you, this recipe is addictive! And be careful, the mandoline is the sharpest tool in the kitchen. Watch your fingertips!

> 2 baking potatoes (about 1 pound), unpeeled
> $\frac{1}{4}$ cup extra-virgin olive oil
> Kosher salt and freshly ground black pepper
> 2 tablespoons chopped fresh chives
> 2 teaspoons chopped fresh marjoram

Using a mandoline or a very sharp knife, cut the potatoes into paper-thin or $\frac{1}{16}$-inch slices and place in a bowl of cold water. Soak for 20 minutes. Drain and completely dry on paper towels or spin dry in a salad spinner.

Preheat the oven to 350°F. Line 3 to 4 baking sheets with parchment paper. Place the potatoes in a bowl and drizzle with the oil. Season well with salt and pepper. Toss well to coat the potatoes thoroughly. Place the potatoes in a single layer on the prepared baking sheets. Bake, turning the potatoes, until golden and crispy, 25 to 30 minutes.

In the meantime, stir the chives and marjoram together. Add 1 teaspoon kosher salt and toss together. When the potatoes are done, place them in a bowl and toss with the herbed salt.

SERVES 6

WINE SUGGESTION: Merlot or Pinot Grigio

> *"New York was his town and always would be."*
>
> WOODY ALLEN

Truffle-Scented Roasted Cornish Hens with Prosciutto and Wild Mushrooms

Cornish hens are great city food. Sometimes called Rock Cornish game hens, they are basically miniature chickens—a cross between a White Rock and a Cornish chicken. They're simple to prepare, extremely versatile, and, when properly cooked, yield succulent, tender meat that falls from the bone. Best of all, each hen weighs approximately one and a half pounds, perfect for a single serving. I like to serve this recipe for special celebrations.

6 Cornish hens (about 1½ pounds each)
Salt and freshly ground black pepper
3 tablespoons unsalted butter
¾ pound wild mushrooms (chanterelles, morels, porcini), finely chopped
1½ teaspoons chopped fresh thyme
3 ¹⁄₁₆-inch-thick slices prosciutto, diced (about 3 to 4 ounces)
3 tablespoons white truffle oil

Remove the neck and giblets from the hens, rinse with cold water, and pat dry. Set aside. Sprinkle the inside with salt and pepper.

Melt 1 tablespoon of the butter in a large skillet over medium heat. Add the mushrooms, season with salt and pepper and the thyme, and cook, stirring occasionally, until soft and the mixture is dry, 3 to 5 minutes. Transfer the mushrooms to a bowl and let cool. Add the prosciutto and truffle oil and stir until mixed.

Inserting your fingertips at the wing end of the breast, gently loosen the skin over the breast and around the thigh and drumstick. Be careful not to tear the skin. Divide the stuffing evenly among the hens. Place one portion of the stuffing under the skin of 1 hen and distribute it evenly over the breast and thigh with your fingers. With kitchen string, tie the legs together at the ankle.

Preheat the oven to 400°F. Arrange the birds breast side up on a rack set in a shallow roasting pan. Melt the remaining 2 tablespoons butter and brush the skin with half of the butter. Sprinkle with salt and pepper. Place the game hens in the oven and roast for 20 minutes. Remove from the oven and brush with the remaining melted butter. Roast until the juices run clear from the thickest part of the thigh and an instant-read thermometer registers 170°F, 25 to 30 minutes longer. Transfer the game hens to a platter and let stand for 10 minutes before serving.

Place 1 hen on each plate and serve.

SERVES 6

WINE SUGGESTION: Barbera, Barolo, or Pinot Noir

Roasted Cornish Hens with Toasted Bread Crumb Salsa

We served a salsa like this at Chez Panisse with everything from rib eye steaks to salmon. Its success depends on the best-quality French or Italian coarse-textured bread crumbs. Toast the crumbs in a 350°F oven, turning occasionally, until golden, 10 to 15 minutes.

6 Cornish hens, halved (1 to 1 1/2 pounds each)

7 tablespoons extra-virgin olive oil

Salt and freshly ground black pepper

2 tablespoons white wine vinegar

1 cup toasted coarse bread crumbs

1/4 cup chopped fresh parsley

1 scallion, white and green parts, thinly sliced

2 anchovy fillets, soaked in cold water for 2 minutes, patted dry, and chopped

1 tablespoon capers, chopped

1 tablespoon grated lemon zest

1 clove garlic, minced

1/2 teaspoon chopped fresh thyme

1/2 teaspoon chopped fresh rosemary

Preheat the oven to 450°F. Arrange the hen halves in a single layer, skin side up, on a baking sheet. Brush the skin with 1 tablespoon of the olive oil and sprinkle with salt and pepper. Roast the hens until an instant-read thermometer inserted into the thickest part of the thigh registers 170°F, 30 to 35 minutes.

Meanwhile, in a bowl, whisk the vinegar and remaining 6 tablespoons olive oil together. Add the bread crumbs, parsley, scallion, anchovies, capers, lemon zest, garlic, thyme, and rosemary and toss together. Season with salt and pepper.

Remove the hens to a platter, top with the toasted bread crumb mixture, and serve immediately.

SERVES 6

WINE SUGGESTION: Sparkling wine, Chardonnay, or Pinot Noir

Fontina, Capocollo, and Roasted Pepper Panini

You'd never guess it from the outside, but Mario's Bohemian Cigar Store in San Francisco is a place where lots of us chefs like to go on our day off. Mario's occupies a tiny corner of Union and Columbus Streets in the heart of North Beach, the city's Italian neighborhood. The best thing to order there is one of the panini, made with focaccia that Mario gets from across the street at the Liguria Bakery, where it comes wrapped in white butcher's paper and tied with string, just like in Italy. Mario's is where I began my obsession with getting an electric panini press so I could make my own panini sandwiches at home. If you don't have a press, substitute a cast-iron ridged grill. (Capocollo is a Calabrian cured meat made with pork and spices. *Capo* means head and *collo* means shoulder. Capocollo comes from the neck of the hog, just in between the two.)

> 3 red bell peppers
> 6 4-inch-square pieces of focaccia, split in half
> 8 ounces Italian fontina cheese, thinly sliced
> 6 ounces capocollo, thinly sliced

Heat an electric panini press or a cast-iron ridged grill.

Place the bell peppers directly over a gas flame or outdoor grill and turn occasionally until black on all sides. Alternatively, cut the bell peppers in half lengthwise and remove the stems, seeds, and ribs, place cut side down on a baking sheet; broil until the skin is blackened, about 10 minutes. Transfer the peppers to a plastic bag, close tightly, and let cool for 10 minutes. Remove the skin by scraping with a knife. Cut the peppers into 1-inch-wide strips and place in a bowl.

Place the bottom half of each piece of focaccia on a work surface in a single layer, cut side up. Divide the fontina into two piles. Using up one pile, distribute the fontina evenly onto the top of the focaccia. Top with the capocollo, distributing evenly. Top the capocollo with the remaining fontina, distributing evenly. Cover the top with the remaining pieces of focaccia.

Place the focaccia sandwiches in the panini press and heat them until golden on the outside and the cheese has melted, 2 to 4 minutes. If you are using the preheated cast-iron ridged grill, cover with a heavy skillet to weight down the sandwich. When the focaccia sandwich is golden on one side, turn the sandwich and continue cooking until golden on the second side and the cheese is melted.

MAKES 6 SANDWICHES

WINE SUGGESTION: Orvieto or Chianti

Panini with Meatballs and Tomato Sauce

This is another great panini recipe and "Mario" favorite. And it's one of mine, too, which isn't really surprising, considering that the comfort food I like best in the whole world is spaghetti and meatballs, a throwback to my childhood. If you've made meatballs and tomato sauce and happen to have some left over, by all means use it here or follow the recipe for Spaghetti and Meatballs (page 192) for another treat!

6 4-inch-square pieces of focaccia, split in half
4 ounces Italian fontina cheese, thinly sliced
4 ounces mozzarella cheese, thinly sliced
6 cups meatballs in tomato sauce (see page 192)

Heat an electric panini press or a cast-iron ridged grill.

Place the bottom half of each piece of focaccia on a work surface in a single layer, cut side up. Divide the fontina into two piles. Repeat with the mozzarella. Using up one pile of fontina, distribute it evenly onto the top of the focaccia. Repeat with one pile of mozzarella. Reserve the remaining fontina and mozzarella. Cut the meatballs in half. Distribute the meatballs and a tablespoon or two of tomato sauce onto the top of the cheese. Top with the remaining fontina and mozzarella. Cover the top with the remaining pieces of focaccia.

Place the focaccia sandwiches in the panini press and heat them until golden on the outside and the cheese has melted, 2 to 4 minutes. If you are using the preheated cast-iron ridged grill, cover with a heavy skillet to weight down the sandwich. When the focaccia sandwich is golden on one side, turn the sandwich and continue cooking until it is golden on the second side and the cheese is melted.

MAKES 6 SANDWICHES

WINE SUGGESTION: Chianti or Pinot Noir

Panini Caprese

Here's a panini recipe that is something of a variation on a classic theme. Take the famous mozzarella, tomato, and basil salad from the Island of Capri and put the ingredients between two pieces of bread. Pop it into a sandwich press, and you have a new classic! And one of Italy's most popular panini.

4 cups basil leaves, washed and spun dry

1/3 cup olive oil

3 cloves garlic, finely minced

4 tablespoons pine nuts, toasted

3/4 cup grated Parmigiano-Reggiano cheese

Salt and freshly ground black pepper

6 4-inch-square pieces of focaccia, sliced in half

1 pound fresh cow's milk mozzarella cheese, thinly sliced

18 thin slices tomato

Salt

Place the basil, olive oil, garlic, and pine nuts in a blender or food processor and blend at high speed until smooth. Stop and scrape down the sides. Add the cheese and pulse a few times to make a good thick paste. Season the pesto with salt and pepper.

Heat an electric panini press or a cast-iron ridged grill.

Place the top and bottom pieces of focaccia on a work surface in a single layer, cut side up. Spread all of the pieces with the pesto, dividing evenly. Divide the mozzarella into two piles. Using up one pile, distribute the mozzarella evenly onto the bottom halves of the focaccia. Place three slices of tomato on top of the cheese. Season with salt. Top each sandwich with the remaining cheese. Cover the tops with the remaining pieces of focaccia.

Place the focaccia sandwiches in the panini press and heat them until golden on the outside and the cheese has melted, 2 to 4 minutes. If you are using the preheated cast-iron ridged grill, cover with a heavy skillet to weight down the sandwich. When the focaccia sandwich is golden on one side, turn the sandwich and continue until it is golden on the second side and the cheese is melted.

MAKES 6 SANDWICHES

WINE SUGGESTION: Orvieto, Est! Est!! Est!!!, or Chianti

"It has been said that all great cities of history have been built on bodies of water—Rome on the Tiber, Paris on the Seine, London on the Thames, New York on the Hudson. If this is a criterion of a city's greatness, surely San Francisco ranks in the first magnitude among cities of the world."

HAROLD GILLIAM

Risotto with Gorgonzola

I just love my job. Maybe because I meet interesting people or because I enjoy traveling so much. Every year I teach in Italy: sometimes in the Veneto; sometimes in Tuscany; sometimes in Sardinia. It seems so unreal that I have to pinch myself. One year I was teaching in the northern part of Italy and was lucky enough to take my students to visit the caves of Gorgonzola. After tasting the authentic creamy, mild, and overwhelmingly delicious Gorgonzola, I went back to the villa and created this recipe with my students.

> 2 tablespoons olive oil
> 1 yellow onion, minced
> ³/₄ cup dry white wine (such as Sauvignon Blanc)
> 6 cups chicken stock
> 2 cups water
> 2¹/₂ cups arborio rice or *vialone nano* rice
> 8 ounces Gorgonzola cheese, crumbled
> ¹/₃ cup milk
> 2 tablespoons butter
> Salt and freshly ground black pepper

Heat the olive oil in a large heavy pot over medium heat. Add the onion and cook, stirring occasionally, until soft, about 10 minutes.

Meanwhile, in a saucepan over low heat, bring the chicken stock and water to just below a simmer.

Add the rice to the onions, increase the heat to medium, and cook, stirring, until the rice is very hot, just begins to stick to the bottom of the pan, and is completely coated with oil, 2 to 3 minutes. Add the wine and cook, stirring, until it has almost evaporated. Add a ladleful of hot chicken stock and stir steadily to keep the rice from sticking. Continue to add more chicken stock a little at a time, stirring until the chicken stock is absorbed and the rice is at the chalky stage, 18 to 22 minutes. Continue to add some of the chicken stock for 2 more minutes, until the rice is just beyond the chalky stage. If you run out of chicken stock, use hot water.

Remove the pan from the heat, add another ladleful of chicken stock, the Gorgonzola, milk, and butter. Season with salt and pepper. Stir quickly, cover, and let sit off the heat for 5 minutes.

After 5 minutes, stir the risotto, season to taste with salt and pepper, and serve immediately.

SERVES 6

WINE SUGGESTION: Fiano di Avellino, Chardonnay, or Sangiovese

RISOTTO 101

When I'm making risotto for company, I'll invite one of my guests into the kitchen and have them stir and add stock. This works at my house, because it's always a cooking class there. But it can work for you, too. People love to help out and be in the kitchen with you.

The other thing I do with risotto is cook it halfway (that is, until half of the liquid has been added). Then I place it on a baking sheet and let it cool in the refrigerator. When I want to serve it, I put it back in the pan and continue to add liquid until it's done. I've cut down my kitchen time by half!

Spaghetti and Meatballs, the Ultimate Comfort Food

Spaghetti and meatballs, also known in my house as "spag and balls," are my absolute favorite comfort food. Whenever I make a batch, I make extra so I can freeze some. This way, when I travel (and that's a lot of the time) I have some comfort food to come home to. The meatballs are inspired by my mother, who I believe makes the best. Hers are so good, in fact, you would think she is Italian. Her secret? Lots of fresh bread crumbs in the meatballs.

SAUCE

2 tablespoons extra-virgin olive oil

5 cups peeled, seeded, and diced tomatoes (fresh or canned)

1 cup water

1 red onion, left whole, peeled

3 tablespoons tomato paste

1 teaspoon sugar

4 basil sprigs

Salt and freshly ground black pepper

MEATBALL AND SPAGHETTI

1 tablespoon extra-virgin olive oil

½ small yellow onion, minced

1 clove garlic, minced

1 cup fresh bread crumbs

½ cup milk

1 pound extra-lean ground beef

1 tablespoon tomato paste

1 teaspoon dried oregano leaves

Salt and freshly ground black pepper

1 pound spaghetti

1 cup freshly grated Parmigiano-Reggiano cheese

Make the sauce: Heat the olive oil in a large pot over medium-high heat. Add the tomatoes, water, onion, tomato paste, and sugar. With the back of a chef's knife, tap the sprigs of basil to release their juices and add to the tomato sauce. Season with salt and pepper and bring to a boil. Reduce the heat to low and simmer until the sauce reduces by one-quarter, about 1 hour. Remove the basil sprigs and onion and discard.

Make the meatballs: Preheat the oven to 400°F. Heat the olive oil in a skillet over medium heat. Add the onion and cook, stirring occasionally, until soft, about 7 minutes.

Add the garlic and cook, stirring occasionally, until the garlic perfumes the air, 30 to 60 seconds. Transfer the onion and garlic to a bowl.

In a bowl, add the bread crumbs and milk and stir together to moisten the bread crumbs. Squeeze the bread crumbs gently and add them to the onion and garlic. Discard the excess milk. Stir in the ground beef, tomato paste, and oregano until well mixed. Season with salt and pepper. Form the mixture into 24 meatballs about $1^1/_4$ inches in diameter. Place on an oiled baking sheet. Bake in the preheated oven until brown on the outside, about 10 minutes.

After the tomato sauce has cooked for 1 hour, add the meatballs and continue to cook until the sauce has reduced slightly and the meatballs are cooked through, 45 minutes. If the sauce gets too thick, add additional water.

Meanwhile, bring a large pot of salted water to a boil. Add the spaghetti and cook until al dente, 8 to 10 minutes. Drain and toss the spaghetti with the tomato sauce and meatballs. Place in a large heated bowl and serve immediately sprinkled with the cheese.

SERVES 6

WINE SUGGESTION: Chianti or Cabernet Sauvignon

Orecchiette with Brussels Sprouts and Bacon

Like beets, Brussels sprouts are in the "love them or hate them" domain of vegetables. I happen to love them, but when I originally developed a variation of this recipe for *Food and Wine* magazine, I wasn't sure how well it would be received. But never before have I received so many compliments from students and friends who made the dish.

  1/2 cup hazelnuts
  1 pound Brussels sprouts, ends trimmed
  3 slices bacon (3 ounces), cut into 1-inch squares
  2 1/2 cups chicken stock
  4 tablespoons unsalted butter
  12 ounces orecchiette pasta
  Salt and freshly ground black pepper
  1 cup grated Parmigiano-Reggiano cheese

Preheat the oven to 375°F. Place the hazelnuts on a baking sheet and bake until light golden, 5 to 7 minutes. Chop coarsely and reserve.

Bring a large pot of salted water to a boil. Add the Brussels sprouts and simmer until tender but crisp, 5 to 7 minutes. Remove from the pan and let cool. When they are cool, cut the Brussels sprouts in half. Reserve.

In a skillet over medium-high heat, cook the bacon, stirring occasionally, until golden and crisp, 7 to 10 minutes. Remove the bacon from the pan and reserve. Do not discard the fat from the pan.

Place the chicken stock in a saucepan and bring it to a boil. Boil until reduced to 1 cup. Reserve.

In a small saucepan over medium-high heat, melt the butter. Heat the butter until the foam begins to subside, it begins to turn brown, and it just starts to smoke and give off a nutty aroma, 3 to 4 minutes. Add the butter to the bacon fat.

Bring a large pot of salted water to a boil. Add the orecchiette and cook until al dente, 12 to 14 minutes.

Meanwhile, heat the butter and bacon fat over medium-high heat. Add the reserved hazelnuts and Brussels sprouts and cook until the Brussels sprouts are hot. Add the reduced chicken stock and remove the pan from the heat. Season with salt and pepper.

To serve, drain the pasta and toss with the Brussels sprouts and their sauce. Sprinkle with the reserved bacon. Place on a platter, garnish with the Parmigiano, and serve immediately.

SERVES 6

WINE SUGGESTION: Sauvignon Blanc or rosé

Oven-Baked Penne with Wild Mushrooms and Fontina

Every once in a while, you have to make a dish that is just plain decadent. Do you have to feel guilty, too? Not if you don't eat the whole thing in one sitting! I always say, "Everything in moderation." And, really, this dish is worth the few extra calories. It's inspired by the pasta dishes of Northern Italy and can be made ahead of time and then baked at the last minute. When you are planning your next dinner party menu, keep this dish in mind— it's a great make-ahead.

½ ounce dried porcini mushrooms

4 tablespoons unsalted butter

2 cloves garlic, minced

1 pound fresh mushrooms, cleaned and halved

Salt and freshly ground black pepper

3 cups half-and-half

3 tablespoons flour

1 cup Parmigiano-Reggiano cheese

1 pound penne

2 tablespoons extra-virgin olive oil

6 ounces fontina cheese, coarsely grated

Place the dried porcini in a bowl. Cover with 1½ cups boiling water and let sit until the water is cool. Drain through a cheesecloth-lined fine-mesh strainer. Place the mushroom-soaking liquid in a saucepan over medium-high heat and reduce to 2 tablespoons; reserve. Chop the mushrooms coarsely.

Melt 1 tablespoon of the butter in a skillet over medium heat. Add the garlic and cook for 1 minute. Add the chopped porcini and the fresh mushrooms and cook until the mushrooms are soft and the liquid from the mushrooms has evaporated, about 5 minutes. Season with salt and pepper and set aside.

Place the half-and-half and the mushroom-soaking liquid in a saucepan and heat until small bubbles form around the edges of the pan. Watch closely. Melt the remaining 3 tablespoons butter in another saucepan over medium heat. Add the flour and cook, stirring constantly for 2 minutes. Stir in the half-and-half mixture and cook, stirring occasionally, until thickened, 3 to 4 minutes. Remove from the heat and stir in half of the Parmigiano. Set aside.

Bring a large pot of salted water to a boil. Add the penne and cook until al dente. Drain and toss with the olive oil, salt, and pepper.

Preheat the oven to 400°F. Butter a 3-quart baking dish. In a large bowl, combine the mushrooms, cream sauce, penne, and the fontina, and stir together. Season with salt and pepper. Pour the mixture into the prepared baking dish. Sprinkle the remaining Parmigiano on top. Cover with aluminum foil and bake for 15 minutes. Remove the cover and bake for 10 minutes longer. Let stand for 5 minutes before serving.

SERVES 6

WINE SUGGESTION: Rosé, Pinot Noir, or Chianti

THE WILDER THE BETTER

Think of fresh mushrooms as sponges that will absorb all of the available liquid. So:

Don't buy wild mushrooms after it's been raining; you'll be paying for rainwater. Do buy them when they're dry.

Don't wash them or soak them in water. I use a damp towel or a mushroom brush to remove any excess dirt or grit. I also trim off the bruised, damaged or dried parts.

Sometimes as a less expensive alternative to wild mushrooms, I'll buy regular white button mushrooms or cremini (they're often sold as wild mushrooms, but they're really cultivated) and get that wild mushroom flavor by adding reconstituted dried wild mushrooms. If I'm making an Italian dish, I'll use dried porcinis; if it's French, dried morels; and if it's Chinese, dried shiitakes.

To reconstitute dried mushrooms: Pour boiling water over the mushrooms to cover and leave the mushrooms in the water until it cools. Remove the mushrooms and squeeze them, saving all the expelled liquid in the bowl. Strain the liquid through a cheesecloth- or paper towel–lined sieve. Use the mushrooms in combination with the fresh mushrooms; the liquid can be added to stocks, soups, or stews.

Green Lasagna with Artichokes and Leeks

When most people think of lasagna, they think of layers of pasta, tomato sauce, ground beef, and ricotta cheese. That's the version our moms made for us when we were kids, right? But there are so many variations. One of my favorites is made with wild mushrooms, leeks, and Gorgonzola cheese. Or this one, made with artichokes and leeks. Granted, lasagna takes some work, but like every great pasta dish, it is so satisfying and well worth it!

1/2 pound lasagna noodles
2 cups (about 1 pound) ricotta
  cheese
3/4 cup freshly grated
  Parmigiano-Reggiano cheese
Salt and freshly ground black
  pepper
2 tablespoons plus 1 teaspoon
  extra-virgin olive oil
5 leeks, white and 3 inches of the
  green parts, cut into 1/2-inch
  dice

1/4 cup lemon juice
4 large artichokes
5 cloves garlic, minced
3 tablespoons unsalted butter
1/4 cup flour
3 cups whole milk
Freshly grated nutmeg
8 ounces mozzarella cheese,
  coarsely grated

Bring a large pot three-fourths full of salted water to a boil. Add the lasagna noodles and cook until al dente, 8 to 12 minutes (refer to the package directions for timing). While the pasta is cooking, fill a large bowl with cold water. When the pasta is done, drain and place in the bowl of water to cool. After 5 minutes, drain the pasta and place the noodles in a single layer on a baking sheet. Cover with plastic wrap and set aside.

In a small bowl mix together the ricotta and Parmigiano. Season with salt and pepper. Set aside.

Heat 2 tablespoons of the olive oil in a skillet over medium-low heat. Add the leeks and cook, stirring occasionally, until very soft and light golden, about 30 minutes. Remove the leeks from the pan and reserve.

Have ready a large bowl of water to which you have added the lemon juice. Cut off the top half of the artichokes, including all of the prickly leaf points. Remove the tough outer leaves of the artichoke until you get to the very light green leaves. Pare the stem to reveal the light green center. If using large artichokes, cut in half lengthwise, then scoop out the prickly chokes and discard. Cut the artichokes, large or small, into thin slices lengthwise. As each is cut, place in the lemon water.

Drain the artichokes and add to the skillet along with $\frac{1}{2}$ cup of water and a large pinch of salt and pepper. Cover and cook over medium heat until the liquid evaporates and the artichokes are cooked through, about 15 minutes. Add the garlic and stir for 1 minute. Add the artichokes to the leeks.

Melt the butter in a saucepan over medium-high heat. Stir in the flour and cook, stirring constantly, for 2 minutes. Add the milk and whisk constantly until it comes to a boil and thickens, 3 to 4 minutes. Season with salt, pepper, and nutmeg.

Preheat the oven to 375°F. Oil a 13 x 9-inch baking dish with the remaining 1 tablespoon olive oil. Cover the bottom of the baking dish with a single layer of the reserved lasagna noodles. Cover the pasta with one third of the ricotta mixture. Sprinkle one third of leeks and artichokes over the ricotta. Spread one third of the sauce over the vegetables. Repeat with 2 more layers. Sprinkle the mozzarella evenly over the top layer. Bake on the top rack of the oven until the top is golden and bubbling around the edges, 40 to 50 minutes. Remove from the oven and let stand for 15 minutes before serving.

SERVES 8 TO 10

WINE SUGGESTION: Pinot Gris, Pinot Grigio, or Sauvignon Blanc

Shanghai Noodles with Chicken, Cashews, Cilantro, and Mint

So much of the really interesting cooking being done in our cities integrates flavors and techniques from disparate cultures. For me, one of the great pleasures and challenges of this kind of cooking is to bring my love of fresh, simple, and seasonal foods to bear on other cuisines, like this recipe that was inspired by a trip to one of San Francisco's three Chinatowns. The ingredients for this particular recipe are pretty straightforward; in fact, you can probably find them in the international section of a well-stocked supermarket.

SAUCE

½ teaspoon ground Szechuan
   peppercorns
½ cup chicken stock
3 tablespoons soy sauce
2 tablespoons Chinese black
   vinegar or balsamic vinegar
2 tablespoon Chinese rice wine
   or dry sherry
2 teaspoons sesame oil
2 teaspoons cornstarch

CHICKEN AND NOODLES

2 skinless and boneless chicken
   breasts (about 12 ounces),
   thinly sliced

3 tablespoons oyster sauce
1 tablespoon soy sauce
1 pound fresh Shanghai-style
   noodles or Chinese egg noodles
½ cup raw cashews
2 tablespoons peanut oil
1 clove garlic, minced
2 teaspoons finely grated fresh
   ginger
1 red bell pepper, thinly sliced
4 scallions, white and green parts,
   thinly sliced diagonally
3 cups baby spinach leaves
½ cup fresh coarsely chopped cilantro
3 tablespoons coarsely chopped
   fresh mint

In a dry pan, toast the Szechuan peppercorns for 30 to 60 seconds.

Make the sauce: In a bowl, whisk together the chicken stock, soy sauce, black vinegar, rice wine, sesame oil, cornstarch, and peppercorns.

Prepare the chicken and noodles: Place the chicken in a bowl with the oyster sauce and soy sauce. Stir together and let stand for 15 minutes.

Bring a large pot of water to a boil. Cook the noodles according to the directions on the package, drain, rinse with cold water, and drain again.

Preheat the oven to 375°F. Place the cashews on a baking sheet and bake until light golden, 5 to 7 minutes. Coarsely chop and set aside.

Place a wok or a wide skillet over high heat until hot. Add the peanut oil and swirl the pan to coat the bottom and sides with oil. Add the garlic and ginger and cook until fragrant, 10 seconds. Add the chicken and stir-fry for 2 minutes. Add the red bell peppers and cook for 1 minute. Add the reserved sauce and cook until the chicken is done and the sauce boils and starts to thicken, about 1 minute. Add the noodles, cashews, scallions, and spinach and toss to coat the noodles. Cook, gently tossing, until heated through. Sprinkle the cilantro and mint on top.

SERVES 6

WINE SUGGESTION: Viognier or Sauvignon Blanc

FAR EAST MEETS WEST

Rice Paper Shrimp Rolls (page 45)
Hot and Sour Soup (page 154)
Thai Beef Salad with Mint and Cilantro (page 128)
Watermelon, Mango, Blueberries, and Lime "Salad" (page 270)

Chicken Lettuce Wraps (page 66)
Shanghai Noodles with Chicken, Cashews, Cilantro, and Mint
    (page 202)
Plum Cake (page 281)

Herb-Crusted Tuna Skewers
with Tomato Aïoli

I have a ton of skewers of all sizes on hand in my kitchen. I find that I can make a simple dinner into something that looks more elaborate by simply skewering the food, whether it is tuna, salmon, halibut, shrimp, scallops, chicken, pork, lamb, beef, or vegetables. Sometimes I serve a few different kinds of skewers with a couple of different sauces. It makes for a fun dinner party and lots of conversation. I've also taken this dish to picnics; it's "shake, rattle, and roll" proof.

2 lemons

1/2 cup olive oil (not extra-virgin)

1 egg yolk

1 teaspoon Dijon mustard

1/2 cup peanut, vegetable, corn, or
   safflower oil

2 cloves garlic, minced

3 tablespoons tomato paste

3 tablespoons water

1 to 2 tablespoons lemon juice

Salt and freshly ground black pepper

1/2 cup chopped fresh parsley

1/3 cup chopped fresh chives

1 tablespoon chopped fresh thyme

1 tablespoon chopped fresh oregano

1 1/2 pounds fresh ahi tuna, cut into
   1-inch chunks

12 lemon wedges, halved

Whole leaves of fresh flat-leaf
   parsley as a garnish

Juice the lemons and place in a container large enough to hold 12 6- to 8-inch skewers. Soak the bamboo skewers in the lemon juice for 1 hour.

Make the aïoli: In a small bowl, whisk 1 tablespoon of the olive oil, the egg yolk, and the mustard together until an emulsion is formed. Combine the remaining olive oil and the peanut oil. Add the oil to the emulsion drop by drop in a steady stream, whisking constantly, until all of the oil has been added. Do not add the oil too quickly and be sure that the emulsion is homogeneous before adding more oil. Add the garlic, tomato paste, and water and mix well. Season to taste with the lemon juice, salt, and pepper.

Heat an outdoor charcoal grill. Alternatively you can heat a nonstick ridged grill pan over medium-high heat for 10 minutes.

On a plate, toss together the parsley, chives, thyme, and oregano on the counter. Skewer the tuna and press the skewers into the herb mixture, coating all sides of the tuna. Place a wedge of lemon on each end. Grill the skewers of tuna, turning every 2 minutes, until cooked but still slightly pink inside, 5 to 7 minutes total.

Remove the tuna skewers from the grill and place on a platter. Garnish with the parsley leaves. Place the aïoli in a small bowl and serve it alongside the tuna.

SERVES 6

WINE SUGGESTION: Any white Rhône wine or rosé

Halibut Parcels with Capers and Lemon Thyme

This dish is a bit of effort, but it's really impressive and sublimely flavorful. Ready the fish packets ahead of time so all you have to do is cook the fish at the last minute. To serve, have your guests use tiny scissors to cut the strings or untie the bows as they would a gift.

FISH

2 pounds halibut fillets, ³/₄ inch thick, skinned and boned

3 tablespoons extra-virgin olive oil

¹/₄ cup minced yellow onion

3 cloves garlic, chopped

1¹/₂ cups fresh bread crumbs

¹/₄ cup capers, chopped

¹/₄ cup finely grated Parmigiano-Reggiano cheese

1 egg, well beaten

1 tablespoon chopped fresh flat-leaf parsley

1 teaspoon grated lemon zest

Salt and freshly ground black pepper

1 lemon

6 bay leaves, halved

VINAIGRETTE AND SPINACH

¹/₄ cup extra-virgin olive oil

2 tablespoons lemon juice

1 teaspoon grated lemon zest

1¹/₂ teaspoons chopped fresh lemon thyme or thyme

Salt and freshly ground black pepper

1¹/₂ pounds baby spinach leaves

6 lemon wedges as a garnish

Prepare the fish: Cut the fish into six 3-inch-square pieces. Split each piece in half, making 12 slices. Chop and reserve the trimmings for the stuffing. Place each slice of fish between waxed paper and pound gently with a meat mallet or a heavy pan until they are about one third again as large.

Heat the olive oil in a skillet over medium-low heat, add the onion and cook until soft, 3 to 5 minutes. Add the fish trimmings and garlic and cook, stirring, for 2 minutes. Add the bread crumbs and stir together over low heat for 30 seconds. Place the mixture

in a bowl with the capers, cheese, egg, parsley, and the lemon zest. Season the stuffing with salt and pepper. Reserve.

Using a vegetable peeler, peel the lemons to make 6 long pieces; reserve.

Place 6 pieces of the halibut on a work surface in a single layer. Place one-sixth of the stuffing on top of each piece of fish. Top with the remaining pieces of fish. Top each bundle with 1 bay leaf and 1 piece of reserved lemon peel. Using cotton kitchen string, tie each parcel around the center in a bow. Place the parcels on an oiled baking sheet.

Make the vinaigrette: In a small bowl, whisk together 3 tablespoons of the olive oil with the lemon juice, lemon zest , and thyme. Season with salt and pepper.

Preheat the oven to 375°F.

Make the spinach: Heat a large skillet over medium heat. Add the spinach and the remaining 1 tablespoon oil. Toss the spinach just until wilted but still bright green, 30 seconds. Season with salt and pepper.

Bake the fish in the oven until done, 20 to 25 minutes.

To serve, place the spinach on the bottom of each plate. Top with one packet of fish. Drizzle the vinaigrette onto the fish and spinach and garnish with lemon wedges.

SERVES 6

WINE SUGGESTION: Grüner Veltliner or Chardonnay

HAPPY BIRTHDAY TO YOU

I love celebrating birthdays. Here is the menu for a birthday party I gave recently. We began with champagne, of course.

Celebration Salad of Endive, Crème Fraîche, and Caviar (page 118)
Halibut Parcels with Capers and Lemon Thyme (page 207)
Caramelized Chocolate Almond Budino (page 266)

Olive Oil–Poached Salmon with Asparagus and Sugar Snap Peas

What a brilliant technique for cooking salmon! I first heard about oil poaching when I read Elizabeth David's cookbooks and then again when I cooked at Chez Panisse. The salmon is cooked ever-so-slowly in fruity olive oil rendering a fully cooked, yet still pink-in-the-center salmon. To accentuate salmon's natural sweetness, I like to sprinkle it with *fleur de sel,* a grayish-colored finishing salt from France, just before serving. This is a spectacular dish for an early spring dinner, when asparagus and sugar snap peas have just come into season.

2 pounds salmon fillet, cut from the middle of the fish, skinned and boned

Extra-virgin olive oil

1 cup shucked sweet peas, fresh or frozen

6 ounces sugar snap peas, cut in half diagonally (1½ cups)

¾ pound asparagus, ends trimmed, cut diagonally into 1½-inch lengths

2 teaspoons lemon juice

1 teaspoon grated lemon zest

1 teaspoon chopped fresh thyme

Salt and freshly ground black pepper

Fleur de sel, optional

Lemon wedges as a garnish

Thyme sprigs as a garnish

Cut the salmon into 6 serving pieces. Place in a deep heavy skillet just large enough to hold the fish. Pour enough olive oil over the fish so that it is just submerged in oil. Place the pan over low heat and cook just until the oil feels warm but not hot (about 100°F on an instant-read thermometer). If white dots appear on the top of the fish during the cooking process, the oil is too hot. Cook until just done and still rosy in the center, 18 to 22 minutes.

Bring a pot of salted water to a boil. Add the sweet peas and cook for 30 seconds. Remove the peas with a slotted spoon and place in a bowl. Add the sugar snap peas to the boiling water and cook until crisp but tender, about 1 minute. Remove with a slotted spoon and add to the peas. Add the asparagus to the water and cook until crisp but tender, 2 to 3 minutes (depending upon the size of the asparagus). Drain and add to the peas and sugar snap peas. Add 2 tablespoons of olive oil and the lemon juice, lemon zest, and thyme to the vegetables; toss together. Season with salt and pepper.

Place a piece of salmon on each plate. Sprinkle with *fleur de sel*. Spoon the vegetables around the salmon and garnish with lemon wedges and thyme sprigs. Serve immediately.

SERVES 6

WINE SUGGESTION: Sauvignon Blanc or Sangiovese

Silver-Roasted Salmon with Sweet-Hot Relish

You'll love this recipe. Not only is it a great technique for cooking salmon perfectly, but the relish—with its great balance of sweet and hot flavors—really accentuates the roasted salmon. Turkish in inspiration, this "sauce" is one of my favorites. I use it not just with salmon, but with any fish or even chicken. It's also great as a dipping sauce for warm grilled bread served with drinks before a meal.

1 side of salmon (2 to 2½ pounds), skinned and boned
Salt and freshly ground black pepper
1 lemon, cut into thin slices
¼ cup extra-virgin olive oil
4 to 5 plum tomatoes (about 1 pound), diced
1 small green bell pepper, diced
½ English cucumber, peeled, seeded, and diced

½ medium onion, diced
2 cloves garlic, minced
2 tablespoons chopped fresh mint
1 teaspoon sweet paprika
⅛ teaspoon cayenne pepper
2 tablespoons lemon juice, plus more if needed
Flat-leaf parsley as a garnish
Lemon wedges as a garnish

Preheat the oven to 400°F. Dry the salmon with paper towels. Rub salt and pepper on both sides of the fish. On a baking sheet large enough to hold the fish, lay an 18 x 30-inch piece of heavy-duty aluminum foil. Lay the fish in the center of the foil. Place the lemon slices on top of the fish. Drizzle 1 tablespoon of the oil over the fish. Cover with a second piece of aluminum foil the same size as the first. Fold and crimp together the edges of both pieces of foil to make an airtight package. Bake the fish until an instant-read thermometer registers 140°F, 25 to 35 minutes.

Heat an outdoor charcoal grill. Alternatively, heat a cast-iron skillet or a ridged grill pan for 10 minutes over medium-high heat. Place the tomatoes and bell pepper on the heat and cook, turning occasionally, until blackened, 4 to 5 minutes. Place the pepper in a plastic bag and let sit 10 minutes. Peel, seed, and dice the pepper. Peel, seed, and chop the tomatoes. Place the tomatoes on a paper towel and let drain for 10 minutes.

In a bowl, combine the tomatoes, bell pepper, cucumber, onion, garlic, mint, paprika, and cayenne. Stir in the remaining 3 tablespoons olive oil and the lemon juice. Season with salt and pepper. Put the mixture in a food processor and pulse 3 times. Season with salt, pepper, and additional lemon juice if needed.

Place the salmon on a platter and cut a slit in the center of the foil. Garnish with the parsley and lemon wedges. Place the sauce in a small bowl and serve on the side.

SERVES 6

WINE SUGGESTION: Chianti

Cedar-Planked Lemon Salmon with Dill

Cooking on a special cedar or alder wood plank is a perfect technique for cooking salmon and other fatty fish. The wood imparts a distinctive aroma and helps keep the fish incredibly moist. Plank cooking isn't some modern innovation; it's been done for generations by Native Americans. The other thing I like about this technique is that it generates a lot of interest and conversation from my guests. Food that has a history and brings a story to the table as well as the dish really interests me.

There are different kinds of planks to use: from those that you soak in water, cook over an open fire, and dispose of after to those that you brush with oil, heat in the oven to a certain temperature, and reuse. While some Native American tribes pass down their planks through the generations, planks can now be purchased at many specialty cookware stores, like Sur La Table.

1½ tablespoons dill seeds	2 tablespoons milk, plus more if
¼ cup olive oil	needed
1 tablespoon lemon-flavored oil	1½ tablespoons chopped fresh dill
2 scallions, white and green	1 tablespoon lemon juice
parts, thinly sliced	Salt and freshly ground black pepper
½ English cucumber, peeled,	2½-pound piece center-cut
halved, seeded, and diced	salmon, skinned and boned
1 cup crème fraîche or sour cream	6 lemon wedges

Place the dill seeds in a small dry skillet over medium heat and cook until fragrant, 30 to 60 seconds. Remove from the pan and place in an electric spice grinder and pulse a few times. Place the dill seeds, olive oil, and lemon oil in a small saucepan and warm slightly. Remove the pan from the heat and let sit for 1 hour. Strain and discard the dill seeds.

Prepare an untreated cedar plank, approximately 17 x 10 inches long, according to the manufacturer's directions. For those that you heat over an open fire, soak it for at least 2 hours and up to 4 hours in cold water. If it floats, weight it down with a brick. Preheat an outdoor grill to medium-high heat, about 400°F. For those that you heat in the oven, brush your plank with oil and heat it in a 350°F oven for 15 minutes.

Meanwhile, in a bowl, combine the scallions, cucumber, crème fraîche, milk, fresh dill, and lemon juice. Season with salt and pepper. If the sauce is too thick, add additional milk.

For the water-soaked plank, remove the plank from the water and place it on the rack of a charcoal grill 5 inches from the heat source until the plank begins to smoke. Brush the salmon with the lemon-dill oil and season with salt and pepper. Place the salmon on the plank, close the lid, and grill until the flesh of the salmon flakes easily with a fork, 20 to 25 minutes.

Alternatively, for the oven-heated plank, remove the hot plank from the oven and place the salmon on top. Brush the salmon with the lemon-dill oil. Sprinkle the salmon with salt and pepper. Roast the salmon in the oven until the flesh of the salmon flakes easily with a fork, 30 to 40 minutes (depending upon the thickness of the fish).

To serve, place the plank on the table, garnished with lemon wedges. Pass the sauce separately.

SERVES 6

WINE SUGGESTION: Chardonnay or Pinot Noir

Salmon with Lemon-Shallot Relish and Crispy Prosciutto

Salmon is so versatile, it seems to work with just about everything. When paired with prosciutto and a tangy vinaigrette spiked with shallots and lemon, its richness is really pronounced. Crispy prosciutto is a snap to make and serves as a wonderful garnish, as well, for salads or soups. It is packed with flavor and provides a nice crunchy texture, especially in this dish.

4 thin slices prosciutto (about 2 ounces)

5 tablespoons extra-virgin olive oil

2 small shallots, minced

2 tablespoons thinly sliced fresh chives

2 tablespoons lemon juice

1 tablespoon grated lemon zest

Salt and freshly ground black pepper

6 1- to 1¼-inch-thick pieces salmon fillet (about 2¼ pounds), skin removed

Lemon wedges as a garnish

Whole leaves of flat-leaf parsley as a garnish

Preheat the oven to 400°F. Cut the prosciutto crosswise into ½-inch strips. Place in a single layer on a baking sheet and bake until crispy and light golden, 7 to 8 minutes. Reserve the prosciutto. Do not wash the pan. Coat the pan with one tablespoon of the oil and reserve for cooking the salmon. Adjust the oven rack to the top third of the oven.

Meanwhile, in a small bowl, whisk together the remaining 4 tablespoons oil and the shallots, chives, lemon juice, and lemon zest. Season with salt and pepper.

Heat a large nonstick skillet over medium-high heat. Add the salmon and cook until light golden on one side, 4 to 5 minutes. Turn the salmon, season with salt and pepper and cook until done, 4 to 5 minutes longer (depending upon the thickness of the salmon).

Place the salmon fillets on serving plates and top with the lemon-shallot relish. Sprinkle the prosciutto on top and garnish with lemon wedges and parsley leaves. Serve immediately.

SERVES 6

WINE SUGGESTION: Pinot Noir or Sangiovese

> *"Most of the family rituals we took for granted were solidly grounded in New York. Looking back, I'm amazed by how many of them had to do with eating. Of course, it is common for New Yorkers to express their connection with the city in culinary terms."*
>
> **CALVIN TRILLIN**

Salmon Burgers with Mustard Mayonnaise

This is a fun alternative to hamburgers and healthier, too. The quality of the roll is crucial, however. Look for a good roll that is crusty on the outside, but tender on the inside. Toast the cut side of the roll; it makes all the difference. I like to cook the salmon in a film of olive oil in a nonstick pan. It renders a crispy golden exterior with a juicy inside, like a perfectly cooked hamburger. Thanks to Jean Tenanes for her continued inspiration.

1/2 cup mayonnaise

1 clove garlic, minced

3 tablespoons capers

2 tablespoons Dijon mustard

1 tablespoon lemon juice

Salt and freshly ground black pepper

1/2 cup olive oil

6 salmon fillets (about 4 to 6 ounces each), skinned and boned

6 good-quality rolls, halved

6 large slices beefsteak tomatoes

3 leaves Bibb lettuce, ribs removed, halved

Place the mayonnaise, garlic, capers, mustard, and lemon juice in a bowl. Mix well and season with salt and pepper.

Place the oil in a heavy nonstick skillet large enough to hold the salmon. Place the pan over medium-high heat. When the oil is hot and almost rippling, add the salmon and cook until golden and crispy on one side, 3 to 4 minutes. Turn the salmon and cook until golden and crispy on the other side, another 3 to 4 minutes.

Toast the rolls on the cut side. Spread with mustard mayonnaise, distributing evenly. Place the bottom part of the roll on a serving plate. Top with a piece of salmon. Top each piece of salmon with a slice of tomato and lettuce. Cover with the top of the roll. Serve immediately.

SERVES 6

WINE SUGGESTION: Rosé or Chardonnay

Pepper-Salt Crabs

This wonderful dish is inspired by the late Barbara Tropp, an incomparable Chinese scholar and chef who founded and cooked at one of the city's most popular and innovative restaurants, China Moon. Barbara loved making this dish with shrimp as well as crab. If you want to make it with shrimp, use one and a half pounds of shrimp still in the shell with their tails on and proceed as you would with the crab.

PEPPER-SALT

1 tablespoon kosher salt

1½ teaspoons Szechuan
   peppercorns

¼ teaspoon five-spice powder

CRAB

6 slices fresh ginger plus
   1 tablespoon finely minced
   fresh ginger

3 scallions, white and green
   parts, cut into 2-inch lengths,
   plus 2 tablespoons finely
   minced scallions

½ cup Chinese rice wine or dry
   sherry

2 whole cooked, cleaned, and
   cracked Dungeness crabs

½ cup all-purpose flour

½ cup water

1 teaspoon baking powder

½ teaspoon kosher salt

4 to 6 cups corn or peanut oil for
   deep-frying

Make the pepper-salt: Combine the salt, peppercorns, and five-spice powder in a dry heavy skillet over medium heat until the salt turns off-white and the peppercorns are fragrant, about 3 minutes. Do not let them scorch. Place the mixture in a mortar and pestle or a electric spice grinder and pulse until the mixture is fine, about 1 minute. Strain through a fine sieve to remove the peppercorn husks and place in an airtight bottle for storage.

Prepare the crab: Place the ginger slices and 2-inch scallion pieces on a work surface. With the handle of a heavy chef's knife or cleaver, smash the ginger and green onions. Place in a large bowl with the rice wine. Add the crabs and refrigerate overnight.

Place the flour, water, baking powder, and salt in a food processor and process until thoroughly mixed, about 1 minute. Add the minced ginger and minced scallion and process until well combined, about 10 seconds. Place in a large bowl and let rest for 1 hour.

About 15 minutes before serving, remove the crab from the marinade. Heat a wok or wide heavy skillet over high heat until hot. Add the oil and heat to 375°F. Place the crabs in the batter and toss to coat. Add the crab to the hot oil in batches and cook until the batter is light golden, 1 to 2 minutes. Drain on paper towels. Repeat with the remaining crab.

Sprinkle the crabs with the pepper-salt, place on a platter, and serve immediately.

SERVES 6

WINE SUGGESTION: Gewürztraminer or Riesling

DUNGENESS CRAB

There are many different species of crab (Blue Crab, King Crab, Snow Crab, and Dungeness Crab are the most familiar to us). Dungeness Crab, with its sweet-tasting, lobster-like meat, is fished up and down the west coast of the United States. It is sold precooked. When you buy crab, look for one that smells sweet and of the sea, and ask your fishmonger to crack it for you.

Clam and Mussel Boil
with Corn and Red Potatoes

I always associate this dish with summer celebrations with my family in New England. We used to make it with lobster, but now that I live on the West Coast, I love to make it with clams and mussels. If you want to add lobster, by all means do so! It can only make your celebration that much merrier. Serve with lots of crusty bread and good beer or a crisp Sauvignon Blanc.

1½ pounds small red potatoes

2 tablespoons extra-virgin olive oil

1 yellow onion, chopped

4 cloves garlic, thinly sliced plus 1 clove garlic, minced

1 cup dry white wine (Sauvignon Blanc)

4 pounds clams, scrubbed well

2 pounds mussels, scrubbed well, beards removed

6 ears of corn, shucked and halved

1 pound green beans, ends discarded, halved

Salt and freshly ground black pepper

2 tablespoons unsalted butter

3 tablespoons chopped fresh flat-leaf parsley

Bring a large saucepan of salted water to a boil. Add the potatoes and cook until done, 7 to 12 minutes (depending upon the size of the potato). Drain the potatoes and set aside.

Warm the olive oil in a large heavy pot over medium-high heat. Add the onion and cook until soft, about 7 minutes. Add the sliced garlic and stir until fragrant, about 1 minute. Add the wine and simmer until the wine has evaporated by half, 5 to 7 minutes. Add the clams, cover, and cook until the clams open, 4 to 6 minutes. Discard any clams that have not opened. With a slotted spoon, transfer the clams to a serving bowl. Add the mussel to the pot, cover, and simmer until they have opened, 3 to 5 minutes. Discard any mussels that have not opened. With a slotted spoon, transfer the mussels to the clam bowl. Cover the bowl with aluminum foil.

Add the corn, green beans, and potatoes to the pot and cook, turning the corn occasionally, until the corn is done and the green beans are tender, 5 to 7 minutes.

With a slotted spoon, remove the corn, green beans, and potatoes and add them to the mussels and clams. Re-cover the bowl with the foil. Boil the liquid in the pot over high heat until it reduces by one third. Season with salt and pepper.

Meanwhile, in a small bowl, mash together the butter, parsley, and minced garlic. Season with salt and pepper.

Pour the reduced liquid over the clams, mussels, corn, green beans and potatoes. Dot the top with the butter and serve.

SERVES 6

WINE SUGGESTION: Sauvignon Blanc, Chardonnay, or Beaujolais

MUSSELS

It's best not to harvest your own mussels as they may be contaminated by pollutants in the water. Instead, buy them from a good fishmonger and look for mussels that are tightly closed or open ones that close when tapped. Just like oysters, they should feel heavy for their size, and they should smell sweet and like the sea. Store in a bowl loosely covered with a damp cloth in the refrigerator up to 24 hours.

To clean and debeard the mussels, scrub them with a stiff brush under cold running water from your tap; just before cooking, remove the beard with a small knife.

Cioppino with Crab, Clams, and Shrimp

For years, the Chinese, Japanese, Hispanics, and Italians have all done their share to add wonderful flavors to the City-by-the-Bay table. Cioppino, a simple shellfish and fish stew, is thought to have been brought to San Francisco in the early twentieth century by the Italians. Its name comes from the word in the Genoese dialect *cioppin,* and translates as "a tasty stew of various qualities of fish." Today cioppino remains a San Francisco treat that pairs well with sourdough bread. The shellfish is left in the shell so you better get out plenty of napkins, bibs, and finger bowls.

You can prepare the base well ahead of time and add the fish at the last minute.

2 cooked Dungeness crabs	2¹/₂ cups tomatoes, peeled, seeded,
¹/₄ cup olive oil	and chopped (fresh or canned)
1 large onion, chopped	1 tablespoon tomato paste
1 small green bell pepper, cut into	2 bay leaves
¹/₂-inch dice	¹/₂ teaspoon dried basil
4 cloves garlic, minced	¹/₄ teaspoon crushed red pepper
1 pound snapper or rock cod, cut	Salt and freshly ground black
into 1-inch pieces	pepper
1 cup dry white wine (Sauvignon	1 pound clams, scrubbed
Blanc)	1 pound large shrimp in their shell
2 cups fish stock or bottled clam	3 tablespoons chopped fresh
juice	parsley as a garnish
2 cups water	

Remove the back shell from the crab and discard. Remove the gills and wash the inside of the crab. Over a bowl, break the crab in half from top to bottom, making two identical halves. Reserve the crab liquid. Cut each half into 3 pieces so that each piece of the body is attached to a leg or claw. Crack the legs and claws.

In a soup pot, heat the olive oil over medium heat. Add the onion, bell pepper,

and garlic and cook, stirring occasionally, until soft, about 10 minutes. Add the crab pieces and crab liquid. Add the snapper and cook slowly, stirring occasionally, for 10 minutes. Increase the heat to high, add the wine and simmer for 3 minutes. Lower the heat and stir in the fish stock and water. Add the tomatoes, tomato paste, bay leaves, basil, and crushed red pepper. Season with salt and pepper and simmer for 10 minutes. Add the clams and shrimp and simmer until the clams open, 3 to 5 minutes. Discard any clams that have not opened. Season with salt and pepper and remove from the heat.

To serve, ladle the cioppino into bowls and garnish with the parsley.

SERVES 6

WINE SUGGESTION: Chianti or Barbera

CLAMS

To clean clams really well, soak them in a bath of heavily salted water in the refrigerator for a few hours or overnight. If you don't have enough time to do this, place them in a bowl and rinse them in several changes of water until no more sand appears on the bottom of the bowl. Or scrub them with a brush.

Pork and Tomatillo Burritos

When I've got the urge for Mexican food, I head straight for La Taqueria or El Metate in the Mission, where they serve the best burritos in the city. With Mexican beer or a glass of fresh mango juice, it's one of the least expensive and most delicious lunches in town. One of the items they don't mention on the menu is the crispy burrito: they take the finished burrito, douse the grill with plenty of oil and roll the burrito in oil until it is crisp on all sides. At La Taqueria, the quintessential condiment for burritos is their fiery hot salsa that sits on every table. When I make burritos at home, I like to garnish them with sour cream, scallions, avocado, and lime wedges.

2 tablespoons vegetable oil

2 pounds boneless pork shoulder
or butt, cut into 1-inch cubes

2 medium yellow onions,
chopped

3 large green bell peppers,
chopped

2 jalapeños, seeded and minced

5 cloves garlic, minced

1½ tablespoons ground cumin

3 cups canned tomatillos, seeded
and chopped

1 cup chopped fresh cilantro

1 cup water

6 large flour tortillas

6 lime wedges

½ cup sour cream

1 avocado, peeled and thinly sliced

3 scallions, white and green parts,
thinly sliced

Fiery Green Salsa (recipe follows)

Heat the oil in a large heavy casserole over medium-high heat. Add the pork in a single layer and brown on all sides, 10 to 12 minutes. Do not overcrowd the pan. Remove the pork from the pan with a slotted spoon. Reduce the heat to medium, add the onions, bell peppers, and jalapeños and cook, stirring occasionally, until the onions are soft, about 10 minutes. Add the garlic and cumin and stir for 1 minute. Add the tomatillos, cilantro, and water. Return the pork to the pot and bring to a boil, then reduce the heat to low, cover, and simmer until the pork is tender, 1½ to 2 hours. Remove the cover and simmer until the sauce thickens and reduces to 1 cup, about 10 minutes.

Preheat the oven to 300°F. Wrap the tortillas tightly in aluminum foil. Heat them in the oven for 15 minutes until hot. One at a time, place one-sixth of the hot filling in the center of each warm tortilla. Roll the tortillas to enclose the filling, leaving the ends open.

Place the burritos on a platter and garnish with the lime wedges. Pass with individual bowls of sour cream, avocado, scallions, and salsa alongside.

SERVES 6

Fiery Green Salsa

2 cups tomatillos, chopped (fresh or canned)

⅓ cup chopped fresh cilantro

¼ cup minced red onion

3 tablespoons fresh lime juice

1 serrano chile, seeded and minced

Salt and freshly ground black pepper

If you are using fresh tomatillos, peel them. Place them directly over the gas flame, on a charcoal grill, or in a heavy dry skillet and cook, turning occasionally, until blackened all over, 5 to 8 minutes. Chop the fresh or canned tomatillos.

In a bowl, stir together the tomatillos, cilantro, red onion, lime juice, and serrano. Season with salt and pepper.

MAKES 2½ CUPS

Pan-Seared Pork Medallions with Riesling and Apples

I like dishes that are seasonal, simple, and assertive. But most important, I like dishes that my guests "ooh and aah" about. This dish, perfect in autumn, is all those things.

1 tablespoon unsalted butter

2 teaspoons brown sugar

2 apples (Jonagold or Sierra Beauty), peeled, cored, and cut into ½-inch slices (about 1¼ pounds)

1 tablespoon safflower, corn, or vegetable oil

2 pork tenderloins, each cut into 6 slices or medallions

Salt and freshly ground black pepper

1 cup late harvest dessert Riesling

⅓ cup raisins

2 cups chicken stock

Melt the butter in large skillet over medium-high heat. Add the sugar and stir until melted. Add the apples in a single layer and cook until golden, 3 to 4 minutes. Turn the apples and continue to cook until done but not falling apart, 2 to 3 minutes.

In another large skillet, warm the oil over medium-high heat until rippling. Add the pork and cook in a single layer until light golden on one side, 4 to 5 minutes. Turn the pork, season with salt and pepper, and continue to cook until done, 4 to 5 minutes. Transfer the pork to a platter. Cover with aluminum foil to keep warm.

Add the wine and raisins to the skillet and increase the heat to high. Reduce the liquid by three-quarters, 2 to 3 minutes. Add the chicken stock and reduce by two thirds or until the sauce thickens and coats a spoon, 10 to 12 minutes.

Pour the sauce into the pan with the apples and heat over high heat until bubbling. Pour the sauce and apples over the pork and serve immediately.

SERVES 6

WINE SUGGESTION: Riesling or Pinot Noir

Lamb Tagine with Artichokes, Preserved Lemons, and Olives

Every once in a while I like to do a dinner that's really exotic. It is times like these that I often turn to North African food. I spent some time in Morocco and particularly loved Marrakech and its exotic, spicy dishes. The word *tagine* actually has two meanings: a savory stew and the vessel the tagine is cooked in. A tagine pot has two pieces: a flat-bottomed, shallow dish and a conical lid. The stew is made directly in the shallow dish and served in it as well. Place the tagine in the middle of your table, remove the lid and dig in! In Morocco, it's customary to use the first three fingers of your right hand to eat directly from the pot. But, of course, you and your guests may use utensils.

2 pounds lamb stew meat, cut from the leg or shoulder, trimmed

1¼ cups minced yellow onion

½ cup chopped fresh parsley

5 cloves garlic, chopped

2 tablespoons vegetable, safflower, sunflower, or corn salad oil

1½ teaspoons sweet paprika

1 teaspoon ground cumin

¼ teaspoon saffron threads

Salt and freshly ground black pepper

4 cups water

½ cup lemon juice

12 small artichokes or 4 medium artichokes

2 Preserved Lemons (recipe follows)

½ cup Kalamata olives, pitted

Fresh cilantro sprigs as a garnish

Place the lamb, onion, parsley, garlic, oil, paprika, cumin, saffron, salt, and ¼ teaspoon pepper in a 5-quart deep casserole. Cover with the water and bring to a boil over high heat. Immediately reduce the heat, cover, and simmer until the meat is very tender and the sauce has reduced to a thick gravy, 1½ to 2 hours. Add water, if necessary, during the cooking time if the sauce gets too thick. Add 2 tablespoons of the lemon juice and season with additional salt and pepper, if needed.

Cut off the top half of the artichoke leaves. Tear off the outside dark and medium green leaves until you get to the light green tender leaves. Trim the torn edges. Trim the stem end. Cut each artichoke in half from top to bottom. If you are using small or baby artichokes they are ready. For medium or large artichokes, using a spoon, scoop out the furry light green choke from the center. Cut into quarters. Place the artichokes in a large bowl of cold water with 4 tablespoons of the lemon juice.

When the lamb is tender, place the artichokes on top. Rinse the preserved lemons and cut into dice. Place on top of the artichokes. Cover and cook until the artichokes are tender, 25 to 30 minutes. Add the olives and sprinkle the stew with the remaining 2 tablespoons lemon juice. Simmer for 2 minutes.

To serve, remove the cover from the *tagine* and garnish with the cilantro.

SERVES 6

WINE SUGGESTION: Cabernet Franc or Cabernet Sauvignon

Preserved Lemons

If Meyer lemons are not available, use Eureka or Lisbon varieties, which are available in any grocery store.

> 8 Meyer lemons, scrubbed
> $\frac{1}{2}$ cup kosher salt
> 2 cinnamon sticks
> 4 bay leaves
> Fresh lemon juice as needed

Cut each lemon into quarters from the top to within $\frac{1}{2}$ inch of the bottom, taking care to leave the 4 pieces joined at the stem end. Sprinkle the insides of the lemon with some of the salt.

Place 1 tablespoon of salt on the bottom of a 1-quart canning jar and pack the lemons into the jar, adding more salt, the cinnamon sticks, and the bay leaves as you go. Push down on the lemons to release as much juice as possible. Add extra lemon juice almost to the top of the jar. Cover the jar tightly. Let the lemons sit at room temperature for 1 month, turning the jar upside down periodically to distribute the salt and juices.

To use the lemons, remove from the brine and discard the pulp. Wash the peel and use. Some white crystals will form on the top of the lemons in the jar, which is normal, so do not discard the lemons. They can be stored at room temperature or refrigerated for up to 1 year.

MAKES 1 QUART

MIDNIGHT AT THE OASIS

Smoked Eggplant with Pita Chips (page 55)

Moroccan Shellfish Cigars (page 81)

Lamb Tagine with Artichokes, Preserved Lemons, and Olives
(page 230)

Your Favorite Couscous

Crispy Moroccan Phyllo with Orange Custard and Almonds
(page 299)

Grilled Lamb Chops with Green and Black Olive Salsa

When you need something really snazzy but easy (say you've been asked to host your brother's birthday party), lamb chops are just the thing. If you cook them right, they will be juicy and full of flavor all by themselves. Add this salsa made with olives, and the olive lovers, like my brother, John, will be in heaven. Yes, I said heaven—right, John?

12 lamb chops (2½ to 3 pounds)

6 tablespoons extra-virgin olive oil

2 anchovy fillets, soaked in water for 2 minutes, then patted dry and minced

⅓ cup cured green olives, pitted and chopped

⅓ cup cured black olives, chopped

⅓ cup green olives with pimento, chopped

1 clove garlic, minced

½ cup fresh chopped flat-leaf parsley

3 tablespoons lemon juice

Salt and freshly ground black pepper

6 lemon wedges as a garnish

Whole leaves of flat-leaf parsley as a garnish

Heat a charcoal grill. Brush the lamb with 1 tablespoon of the olive oil.

In a small bowl, combine the anchovies, olives, garlic, parsley, and lemon juice. Stir in the remaining 5 tablespoons olive oil. Season to taste with salt and pepper.

Place the lamb chops on the grill and grill until golden on one side, 4 to 6 minutes. Turn, season with salt and pepper, and cook until golden and medium rare on the second side, 4 to 6 minutes (depending upon the thickness of the lamb chops).

Place two lamb chops on each plate and top with the olive salsa. Garnish with lemon wedges and parsley and serve immediately.

SERVES 6

WINE SUGGESTION: Shiraz or Cabernet Sauvignon

Roulade of Herbed Lamb with Stewed Garlic

The herbs rolled in this loin of lamb are basically a fresh combination of *herbes de Provence,* the flavorful mix of herbs often associated with the south of France. Serve the lamb with Olive Oil–Mashed Potatoes (page 238) and Minted Sugar Snap Peas (page 238) or young green beans, depending upon the season. This is a meal to impress your friends and one that might be served in a fine city restaurant.

3 boned racks or loins of lamb, fat removed

Salt and freshly ground black pepper

1/2 cup chopped fresh parsley

1/4 cup chopped fresh chives

2 tablespoon chopped fresh mint

1 tablespoon chopped fresh rosemary

1 tablespoon lavender flowers, fresh or dried

1 teaspoon chopped fresh thyme

1 teaspoon chopped fresh oregano

1/4 cup extra-virgin olive oil

1 tablespoon unsalted butter

30 medium cloves garlic, peeled

10 cups (2 1/2 quarts) homemade chicken stock

1 pound lamb stew meat, fat removed, cut into 1/2-inch cubes

1 teaspoon cornstarch

Parsley, mint, rosemary, thyme, or oregano sprigs as a garnish

Fresh lavender sprigs as a garnish

Make a 1/2-inch-deep cut along the long side of the lamb rack or loin to butterfly the meat. Continue to cut deeper and deeper into the rack or loin in a circular pattern, creating a flat piece. Season with salt and pepper. Pound the meat slightly to flatten evenly.

In a bowl, combine the parsley, chives, mint, rosemary, lavender, thyme, and oregano. Sprinkle with salt and pepper and 1 tablespoon of the olive oil. Mix well. Spread the mixture evenly over the flattened lamb. Roll the lamb back up to its original shape, enclosing the herbs. Tie with kitchen string at 1-inch intervals. Refrigerate the lamb. Note: This can be done up to 1 day in advance.

Heat 1 tablespoon of the olive oil and the butter in a skillet over medium heat, add the garlic, and cook, stirring occasionally, until light golden, about 15 minutes. Add 2 cups of the chicken stock and simmer over low heat until the garlic is soft, 15 to 20 minutes. With a slotted spoon, remove the garlic from the stock and reserve the garlic and stock separately.

Heat 1 tablespoon of the olive oil in a large skillet over medium heat. Add the lamb stew cubes and cook, turning occasionally, until golden brown on all sides, 20 to 30 minutes, being careful not to burn. Add the reserved garlic stock and simmer gently over medium-low heat until the liquid has reduced by half, about 10 minutes. Add 4 cups chicken stock and reduce slowly by half, 15 to 20 minutes. Add the remaining 4 cups chicken stock and reduce by one-quarter until the sauce coats the back of a spoon lightly, 10 to 15 minutes. Strain the sauce into a saucepan and discard the lamb pieces. In a small bowl, whisk together the cornstarch and 1 tablespoon water. Bring the sauce to a boil. Slowly whisk in enough of the cornstarch mixture so the sauce coats the back of a spoon. Add the reserved garlic cloves, season with salt and pepper, and set aside.

Bring the lamb loins to room temperature. Preheat the oven to 425°F.

Heat the remaining 1 tablespoon olive oil in an ovenproof skillet over high heat. Brown the lamb loins, turning occasionally, until golden on all sides, 6 to 8 minutes total. Transfer the pan to the oven and cook until medium rare and the internal temperature is 140°F, 8 to 10 minutes. Let rest for 5 to 10 minutes before slicing.

To serve, slice each lamb loin into 6 1-inch-thick pieces, removing the strings as you go. Place 3 pieces of lamb on each plate and distribute the sauce and garlic cloves around the lamb. Garnish with sprigs of herbs and lavender.

SERVES 6

WINE SUGGESTION: Shiraz, Syrah, or Côtes du Rhône

Olive Oil–Mashed Potatoes

3 pounds red potatoes, peeled and quartered

$^1\!/_3$ cup heavy cream

$^1\!/_4$ cup extra-virgin olive oil

$^1\!/_4$ cup snipped fresh chives

2 tablespoons unsalted butter, at room temperature

2 tablespoons white wine vinegar

Salt and freshly ground black pepper

Put the potatoes in a pot of salted water and bring to a boil. Boil until tender, 20 to 30 minutes. Drain and return to the saucepan.

Heat the heavy cream in a small saucepan until warm. Add the cream to the potatoes. Over low heat, add the olive oil, chives, butter, and vinegar and mash with the potatoes and cream. Season to taste with salt and pepper.

SERVES 6

Minted Sugar Snap Peas

$1^1\!/_2$ pounds sugar snap peas, ends trimmed

$1^1\!/_2$ teaspoons unsalted butter

$1^1\!/_2$ teaspoons extra-virgin olive oil

1 tablespoon chopped fresh mint

Salt and freshly ground black pepper

Bring a large pot of salted water to a boil. Add the sugar snap peas and simmer until bright green and crunchy, 1 to 2 minutes. Drain and run under cool water.

In a skillet over medium heat, melt the butter in the olive oil. Add the sugar snap peas and cook, stirring occasionally, until hot, about 1 minute. Add the mint and season to taste with salt and pepper. Stir together and serve immediately.

SERVES 6

NEVER ENOUGH PLATTERS

Sometimes I love family-style platters for serving, especially when I want the meal to feel like a family dinner (even if it's friends). I'll pick out one of my big, Italian handpainted majolica platters for the main course and set it in the middle of the table along with a couple of large serving pieces for the vegetables and starch, and then gather everybody around.

Sometimes, though, I prefer a more formal style (this probably goes back to my restaurant training). At these times, I like to plate each dish. As a rule of thumb, I'll do this for dinner parties of six to eight people. Plating for ten or twelve can be a little daunting if you're doing it yourself, so I'll serve family style. Or, if I have a large group, sometimes I'll plate the salad and then serve the main course family style. I like to mix it up.

Spiced Lamb Sausage with French Lentils

There is a tiny, lunch-box of a restaurant called La Merenda just off the Cours Seleya market in Nice, one of the very best Provençal cities in France, that serves this fantastic stew: spiced lamb sausages simmered in a richly flavorful tomato and lentil sauce. When you make it, it is best to use the tiny, superior, blue-green du Puy French lentils. But if you can't find them, use our gray-green, grocery store variety. In either case, don't presoak the lentils and cook them just until they are tender; never cook them until they fall apart. A perfect make-ahead dish, this can be prepared up to a day in advance and stored in the refrigerator.

LAMB SAUSAGE

2 teaspoons sweet paprika

1¼ teaspoons ground cumin

½ teaspoon ground coriander

½ teaspoon cinnamon

¼ teaspoon cayenne pepper

¼ teaspoon ground cardamom

¼ teaspoon ground cloves

1 pound lean lamb meat (leg or
   shoulder), cut into chunks

¼ pound pancetta, minced

½ cup fresh bread crumbs

¼ cup milk

4 cloves garlic, minced

3 tablespoons chopped fresh mint

2 tablespoons chopped fresh flat-
   leaf parsley

2 teaspoons chopped fresh oregano

Salt and freshly ground black
   pepper

SAUCE

3 cups tomatoes, peeled, seeded,
   and chopped (fresh or canned)

1¼ cups green lentils

3 tablespoons extra-virgin olive oil

1 small yellow onion, diced

1 very small carrot, diced

20 cloves garlic

1 quart chicken stock

4 sprigs flat-leaf parsley, tied
   together

2 bay leaves

¼ cup chopped fresh mint as a
   garnish

Make the lamb sausage: In a small dry skillet over high heat, heat the paprika, cumin, coriander, cinnamon, cayenne, cardamom, and cloves until aromatic, about 30 seconds. In a bowl, combine the spices with the lamb, pancetta, bread crumbs, milk, garlic, mint, parsley, oregano, 1 teaspoon salt, and ½ teaspoon black pepper and mix well.

Grind the mixture in a food processor until half is very fine and half is coarse. Test one for flavor by frying a small flattened sausage on both sides in a skillet over medium-high heat until cooked through, about 5 minutes. When it has cooled, taste and season the sausage mixture with more salt, pepper, and spices, if needed. Divide the mixture into 24 small slightly flattened sausages. Refrigerate until ready to use.

Make the sauce: Drain the tomatoes, reserving 1 cup of juice. Chop the tomatoes very coarsely. Measure out 1 cup and reserve.

Pick over the lentils and discard any stones or damaged lentils. Rinse well.

In a large skillet, heat 2 tablespoons of the olive oil over medium heat. Add the onion, carrot, and garlic cloves and cook, stirring occasionally until the onions are soft, 7 minutes. Add the lentils and stir to coat with the olive oil, for 2 or 3 minutes. Add the reserved tomato juice, chicken stock, parsley, and bay leaves and bring to a boil. Turn the heat to low and simmer gently until the lentils are tender and the liquid has reduced, about 1 hour.

Meanwhile, heat the remaining 1 tablespoon olive oil in another skillet over medium-high heat. Add the sausage and cook until light golden, 1 minute per side. Do not overcrowd the pan.

When the lentils are done, discard the parsley sprigs and bay leaves. Add the sausages to the lentils and simmer over low heat until the sausages are cooked through, about 15 minutes. Add the tomatoes and continue to cook for 10 minutes. Season to taste with salt and pepper.

Place the lentils on a serving plate and top with 4 sausages. Garnish with the remaining chopped mint and serve immediately.

SERVES 6

WINE SUGGESTION: Shiraz, Syrah, Châteauneuf-du-Pape, or Côtes du Rhône

Golden-Sautéed Veal with Arugula and Tomato Salad

I first became acquainted with this dish many years ago when I visited Lucca, Tuscany where I cooked for a few days with Nonna, the 70-year-old grandmother chef, at the Antico Locando, a little roadhouse trattoria elegantly nestled by the side of the road. Nonna was a fabulous cook. This is a dish we cooked together and enjoyed as a late lunch that first day. She told me that chicken breasts may be substituted for veal in this make-ahead dish. Bread the veal hours in advance and, at the last minute, cook the veal and toss the salad. *Perfetto!* You have a simple, flavorful dish for a quick family supper.

1¼ pounds veal scallopine, cut
   from the sirloin
3 tablespoons extra-virgin olive
   oil
1½ tablespoons lemon juice
1 small clove garlic, minced
Salt and freshly ground black
   pepper

½ cup all-purpose flour
2 eggs, beaten lightly together
2 cups dry bread crumbs
1 tablespoon unsalted butter
3 cups very coarsely chopped
   arugula
2 small tomatoes, diced
Lemon wedges as a garnish

Pound each piece of veal between two pieces of waxed paper with a large flat meat mallet until even.

In a small bowl, whisk 2 tablespoons of the olive oil with the lemon juice and garlic. Season with salt and pepper. Reserve.

To bread the veal, place the flour in one bowl, the eggs in another bowl, and the bread crumbs in a third bowl. Season the eggs and bread crumbs with salt and pepper and stir together to mix well. Coat both sides of the veal with the flour, shaking off the excess. Next, coat the veal with the egg, letting the excess drain. Finally, coat both sides of the veal lightly with the bread crumbs and pat off the excess.

In a large skillet, heat the remaining 1 tablespoon olive oil and the butter over medium-high heat. Add the veal pieces in a single layer. Do not overcrowd the pan. Cook the veal pieces, turning occasionally, until golden brown on each side, 4 to 6 minutes total.

Place the veal on a platter. Toss the arugula and tomatoes with the reserved vinaigrette. Top the veal with the salad and serve immediately, garnished with lemon wedges.

SERVES 6

WINE SUGGESTION: Grüner Veltliner, Beaujolais, or Pinot Noir

"Chicago is a great American city."

NORMAN MAILER

Braised Veal Shanks
with Olives and Lemon

I have been teaching in Australia for years and absolutely love it, especially in Sydney. One of my favorite chefs there, Janni Kyritsis, a Greek expatriate and dear friend, makes some of the most wonderful Mediterranean-inspired food. Last time I was there, he made me this dish for dinner. Before I arrived home, he had already emailed the recipe to me! I am thrilled to include it here.

VEAL

3 tablespoons extra-virgin olive oil

12 veal shanks, on the bone
   (approximately ¹/₂ pound each)

18 pearl onions, peeled

2 yellow onions, chopped

2 carrots, chopped

2 stalks celery, chopped

1 cup dry white wine

1 quart chicken stock

10 sprigs thyme

6 sprigs parsley

3 3-inch pieces lemon peel, white
   pith removed

Salt and freshly ground black
   pepper

12 cloves garlic

1 lemon, thinly sliced

24 green Picholine or Lucques
   olives

GARLIC SAUCE

¹/₂ cup whole almonds, toasted

4 garlic cloves

¹/₄ cup water, plus more if needed

1 egg yolk

1 tablespoon lemon juice

¹/₂ cup extra-virgin olive oil

¹/₂ cup fresh bread crumbs

Salt and freshly ground black
   pepper

GARNISH

¹/₂ cup chopped fresh flat-leaf
   parsley

1 clove garlic, minced

1 tablespoon grated lemon zest

Orzo (recipe follows)

Prepare the veal: Preheat the oven to 300°F. Warm the olive oil in a large heavy pan over medium-high heat. Add the veal and cook, turning occasionally, until brown on all sides, about 12 minutes. Remove from the pan and reserve. Add the pearl onions to the pan and cook, stirring occasionally, until light golden, 4 to 6 minutes. Remove from the pan and reserve separately from the veal. Add the yellow onions, carrots, and celery to the pan and cook, stirring occasionally, until the vegetables are tender, about 10 minutes. Increase the heat to high, add the white wine, and stirring with a wooden spoon, cook until the wine is reduced by half, 2 to 3 minutes. Add the veal back to the pan, along with the chicken stock, thyme, parsley, lemon peel, salt and pepper. As soon as it comes to a boil, cover the pan and braise in the oven until the veal is tender, 1½ hours.

Make the garlic sauce: Place the almonds and garlic in a food processor and process to make a paste. Add the water, egg yolk, and lemon juice and process for 10 seconds. Add the oil slowly, drop by drop, until all of it has been added. Add the bread crumbs and pulse to make a smooth paste. Season with salt and pepper. As it sits, the sauce has a tendency to thicken; if so, add additional water to loosen.

After the veal has cooked for 1½ hours, strain the cooking liquid, pressing as much of the liquid out of the vegetables as possible. Discard the vegetables. Add the garlic cloves, lemon slices, green olives, and pearl onions to the broth. Cover and bake until the meat falls off the bone, about 1 hour. Taste. If the liquid is too thin and tasteless, place 2 cups in a saucepan and reduce until thickened. Pour the liquid back into the veal pan and stir to mix. Season with salt and pepper.

Make the garnish: In a bowl, combine the parsley, garlic, and lemon zest. Reserve.

To serve, place the orzo onto a platter and make a well in the center. Spoon the veal, vegetables, and broth into the center. Sprinkle the reserved garnish on top. Spoon a heaping spoonful of the garlic sauce onto the top and serve. Pass the remaining sauce in a bowl on the side.

SERVES 6

WINE SUGGESTION: Chianti or Pinot Noir

Orzo

12 ounces orzo

2 tablespoons unsalted butter

1 small yellow onion, minced

Salt and freshly ground black pepper

Bring a large pot of salted water to a boil. Add the orzo and simmer for 2 minutes. Drain.

In a skillet over medium heat, melt the butter. Add the onion and cook until soft, about 10 minutes. Add the orzo and stir together. Season with salt and pepper.

SERVES 6

Napolitan Braised Beef Ragu in Two Courses

I have always loved Paul Bertolli's cooking. When I worked at Chez Panisse, he was the chef in the downstairs Restaurant. Everyone tries to cook Italian, but I have always thought Paul's food was the closest to Italy this side of the Atlantic. This dish was inspired by him. What I love about it is that it can be served in two courses. For a first course, toss the pasta with the hot sauce and top with freshly grated Parmigiano-Reggiano cheese. For the main course, serve the beef with your favorite vegetables. I like green beans, eggplant, or roasted potatoes.

4 cups water

½ ounce dried porcini mushrooms

1 tablespoon olive oil

3½ pounds beef chuck

Salt and freshly ground black pepper

3 ounce slice pancetta, diced

1 carrot, finely diced

1 stalk celery, finely diced

1 medium yellow onion, finely diced

3 cups peeled, seeded, and diced tomatoes (fresh or canned)

½ cup tomato paste

2 teaspoons sugar

5 cloves garlic, minced

1 pound penne or rigatoni

Freshly grated Parmigiano-Reggiano cheese

Bring the water to a boil and pour over the porcinis. Let sit until the water is cool.

Heat the olive oil in a large heavy casserole over medium heat. Season the meat with salt and pepper and add to the pan and cook, turning occasionally, until golden brown and caramelized on both sides, about 20 minutes. Remove the meat from the pan and set aside.

Add the pancetta to the pan and cook, stirring occasionally, until light golden, about 10 minutes. Add the carrot, celery, and onion to the pan and cook, stirring occasionally, until the vegetables begin to soften and turn golden, about 15 minutes. Strain the porcinis, reserving the mushrooms and liquid separately. In a large bowl, stir together the tomatoes, tomato paste, sugar, and the porcini soaking liquid.

Add the porcinis and garlic to the pan. Increase the heat to high and stir in the tomato mixture. Add the meat back into the pan. Bring to a boil, reduce the heat to low and simmer, turning the meat occasionally, until the meat is tender, $2\frac{1}{2}$ to 3 hours. (To see if the meat is tender, insert a knife into the center—there should be no resistance.) If the sauce thickens too much, add water.

Remove the meat from the pan and cover with aluminum foil. Puree the sauce in a blender or food mill until smooth. Season with salt and pepper.

Cook the pasta in boiling salted water until tender. Toss the pasta with as much sauce as needed. Serve with grated Parmigiano for the first course.

Slice the meat and serve with the sauce for the main course.

SERVES 6

WINE SUGGESTION: Chianti, Barolo, Barbera, or Dolcetto

Soy-Marinated Flank Steak with Asian Pesto

Inspired by my dear friend and chef, Bibby Gignilliat, this dish is a wonderful example of city food: flavorful, simple, and exciting. Bibby contends that it has be served with Wasabi-Mashed Potatoes (page 251).

FLANK STEAK

2½ pounds flank or skirt steak

2 cups soy sauce

1 clove garlic, sliced

1 tablespoon ginger, minced

1 tablespoon brown sugar

1 teaspoon canola oil

PESTO

3 scallions, white and 3 inches of the green part, coarsely chopped

½ cup cilantro leaves

½ cup fresh flat-leaf parsley leaves

2 tablespoons extra-virgin olive oil

2 tablespoons pine nuts, toasted

1 teaspoon sesame oil

1 clove garlic, sliced

1 tablespoon sesame seeds, toasted

Salt and freshly ground black pepper

Prepare the flank steak: Preheat the oven to 400°F. Trim the silver skin and excess fat from the flank steak. With the tip of the knife, score each side of the meat. In a bowl, whisk together the soy sauce, garlic, ginger, brown sugar, and canola oil. Place the steak in a large baking dish and pour the marinade over the steak. Cover the baking dish with plastic wrap and refrigerate the steak for at least 4 hours or overnight. Let the steak return to room temperature before grilling.

Make the pesto: In a food processor, combine the scallions, cilantro, parsley, olive oil, pine nuts, sesame oil, and garlic. Process until smooth. Stir in the sesame seeds. Season with salt and pepper.

Preheat an outdoor grill, an indoor cast-iron ridged grill pan, or a large skillet. If you are using a grill pan, heat the grill over medium-high heat for 10 minutes. Remove the steak from the marinade and scrape off most of the marinade. Brush the grill with oil; then sear the flank steak on both sides until golden brown in color. Transfer the browned steak to a baking sheet, and finish cooking in the oven until medium rare and an instant-read thermometer registers 135°F, 10 to 15 minutes. Let rest for 5 minutes, covered loosely with aluminum foil, before slicing and serving.

To serve, thinly slice the flank steak and place on a platter. Top with the pesto.

SERVES 8

WINE SUGGESTION: Riesling or Cabernet Sauvignon

Wasabi-Mashed Potatoes

2 1/2 pounds baking potatoes, peeled and cut into 1-inch pieces

1/2 cup milk

2 teaspoons wasabi powder

2 tablespoons unsalted butter

2 teaspoons white wine vinegar

Freshly ground black pepper

Salt

Bring a large pot of salted water to a boil. As you peel and cut the potatoes, put them in a large bowl of cold water. When all the potatoes have been peeled, drain the potatoes and add them to the boiling water. Boil until completely tender, about 20 minutes. Reserve 1 cup of the cooking liquid, then drain the potatoes. Set aside.

Combine the milk and wasabi powder in a small bowl and stir to dissolve the powder.

Using a food mill or ricer, mash the potatoes into a clean pot. Stir in the wasabi milk, butter, and vinegar. Season with pepper. Add as much of the reserved potato liquid to loosen the potatoes as needed. Season with salt and pepper.

SERVES 6

City Entertaining

E verything, everything, that I think about city food—that it should be bright, fresh, flavorful, dazzling, generous, even lusty and, above all, simple—goes for city entertaining. Casual isn't quite the right word; or informal. It's more like gracious, spontaneous, easy, a balance of the sublime and the spectacular that extends from the first course straight through to the final pleasure of the table: dessert.

"People always come for the dessert," my mother used to say of entertaining. We want to be tempted by it, and, aware of it or not, we always save room for it. So I try to bring all of the same discernment to my choice of dessert that I do to all of the courses that precede it. The dessert should complement the rest of the meal, yet be surprising and have just the right balance of flavor, texture, and color. It should incorporate the highest quality, seasonal ingredients (whether it's chocolate, fruits, berries, or nuts). And it should be beautiful, but not showy, so that it is the perfection of the flavors you have combined that delights and satisfies and not the mere presentation of them.

Of course, this is the balance that I am always striving for in every dish and in the style of my table and home when I entertain. I try not to set my table as though it's a stage on which my dinner will debut but to have it express warmth and pleasure.

I like colorful, simple linens. And I like to use candles and flowers and other natural elements to intensify the consciousness of the season.

I realize this may just be my own personal style. (I admit I don't even own a white tablecloth and my silver candlesticks are pewter or Italian handpainted majolica.) But I really believe that this way of entertaining is in sync with city life and also that it opens people to the experience of the table, the food, and each other.

There *are* special challenges to entertaining in a city, where the pace of living is just a bit too fast, so here are my top ten tips for easier, effortless, and artful entertaining:

1. Plan ahead.
2. Prepare everything in advance that you possibly can (this includes food and table settings).
3. Don't skimp: buy the best you can afford and lots of it.
4. Practice: never serve a dish you haven't mastered.
5. Never, *never* apologize for the food.
6. Always have a story to tell about the food or the wine you serve.
7. Invite wonderful, interesting people.
8. Don't be bound by the boy/girl/boy/girl seating rule.
9. If you're entertaining outdoors, always have a backup plan in case the weather turns on you.
10. Make sure your dessert is worth coming for.

Individual Warm Raspberry Soufflés

All of my best parties have been elevated by the presence of Gary Danko, my friend and the chef and owner of his extraordinary namesake restaurant in San Francisco. These beautiful soufflés were inspired by him and meet all my criteria for city entertaining—luscious and elegant! And best of all, they're absolutely incredible to eat but not too rich.

SOUFFLÉS

2 teaspoons butter

2 tablespoons sugar

³/₄ cup excellent-quality
raspberry jam, strained and at
room temperature

6 egg whites

1 tablespoon kirsch

SAUCE

2 cups fresh (or frozen, defrosted)
raspberries

1 tablespoon sugar

1 tablespoon kirsch

Make the soufflés: Preheat the oven to 375°F. Grease 10 ¹/₂-cup soufflé dishes with the butter. Dust lightly with the sugar and tap out the excess. Place the soufflé dishes on a baking sheet.

Strain the raspberry jam through a fine-mesh strainer. Place the egg whites in a bowl and warm the whites directly over the burner of the stove, swirling the bowl until the whites are just warm to the touch. Whip the whites to stiff peaks. Fold the jam and kirsch into the whites with as few folds as possible. Pour the mixture into the prepared soufflé dishes and bake until well puffed and the center does not shake when lightly jiggled, 10 to 15 minutes.

Meanwhile, make the sauce: Puree the raspberries in a food processor until smooth. Strain. Stir in the sugar and kirsch.

Serve the soufflés immediately and pass the sauce on the side. To serve the sauce, cut a hole into the center of each soufflé and pour the sauce into the center.

SERVES 10

Panna Cotta with Raspberries

In Italian, *panna cotta* means "cooked cream." Like all custards, I think that makes it a great choice for adults and children alike. So when my brother, John, and his son, Cory, came into the city recently for dinner, I made *panna cotta* for dessert, and knowing that my brother loves vanilla like I do, I put lots of vanilla bean into the custards. As I turned the custards out onto the serving plates, my nephew asked why I put all that black pepper into the *panna cotta*. It was just all the little vanilla seeds! Despite the "pepper," they both absolutely loved the dessert. I adapted this recipe from one by Nancy Silverton of Campanile in Los Angeles. She is a fantastic pastry chef, baker, and, in food circles, well known for her creamy *panna cotta*.

CUSTARDS

2 tablespoons cold water

1³/₄ teaspoons unflavored
    powdered gelatin

1¹/₂ cups heavy cream

¹/₂ cup milk

4 tablespoons sugar

Pinch of salt

2 vanilla beans

SAUCE

2 cups raspberries

3 tablespoons water

2 tablespoons sugar

1 tablespoon kirsch

1 teaspoon lemon juice

Make the custards: Place the water in a small bowl. Sprinkle the gelatin over the water and set aside until softened, about 5 minutes.

Place the cream, milk, 3 tablespoons of the sugar, and the salt in a saucepan. With a small knife, cut halfway through the vanilla bean lengthwise. Open the vanilla bean and scrape the seeds into the pot. Add the beans to the vanilla mixture. Bring to a boil over high heat, reduce to medium heat, and boil for 1 minute, stirring constantly. Watch closely so it doesn't boil over. Remove the pan from the heat and whisk in the remaining 1 tablespoon sugar and the gelatin mixture until dissolved.

Strain the cream through a fine-mesh strainer; discard the vanilla beans. Chill in the refrigerator or over an ice bath just until cool and slightly thicker than heavy cream, but not set. Pour into 6 5-ounce ramekins. Refrigerate for 3 hours.

Make the sauce: Puree 1¼ cups of the raspberries in a blender with the water, sugar, kirsch, and lemon juice. Strain through a fine-mesh strainer. Place in a bowl and add the remaining ¾ cup raspberries; stir together.

Just before serving, run a small knife around the edge of each ramekin. Unmold the panna cotta onto serving plates and spoon the sauce around the custards.

SERVES 6

"*Rome was a poem pressed into service as a city.*"

ANATOLE BROYARD

Warm Polenta Custards with Grappa-Soaked Golden Raisins

Comfort desserts are my favorite. Sometimes this means fruit desserts; sometimes it means warm desserts; and sometimes it means custardy desserts. This one fits the bill in every way. Serve it when the weather cools in late autumn.

STEWED FRUIT

2 cups port

1/4 cup honey

5 whole cloves

1 2-inch strip orange zest, white pith removed

3 slices fresh ginger

1 cup dried apricots (about 3 ounces)

1 cup pitted dried plums or prunes (about 3 ounces)

1/2 cup grappa

1/4 cup golden raisins

CUSTARD

2 1/4 cups milk

1/8 teaspoon salt

3/4 cup polenta

8 ounces ricotta

6 tablespoons granulated sugar

1/4 teaspoon cinnamon

3 eggs

1/2 cup crème fraîche, lightened with 1 to 2 tablespoons milk

Confectioners' sugar

Make the stewed fruit: Place the port, honey, cloves, orange zest, and ginger in a saucepan over high heat and bring to a boil. Reduce the heat to low, add the apricots, and simmer until they being to soften, 5 to 10 minutes. Add the dried plums and continue to simmer until the apricots and dried plums are soft, about 10 minutes. Remove the ginger, orange zest, and cloves and discard. Reserve.

Heat the grappa in a saucepan until it is hot. Remove from the heat, add the raisins, and let sit for 30 minutes.

Make the custard: Bring the milk and salt to a boil in a large saucepan over high heat. Lower the heat to medium and slowly add the polenta, whisking constantly.

Continue to whisk the mixture for 2 to 3 minutes. Change to a wooden spoon and simmer, stirring periodically until the spoon almost stands in the polenta, 10 to 15 minutes.

Preheat the oven to 375°F. Mix the ricotta and granulated sugar together in a large bowl. When the polenta is cooked, immediately add the polenta to the ricotta and stir until well mixed. Drain the raisins, discard the grappa, and add them to the polenta with the cinnamon. Whisk the eggs together in a small bowl and add them to the polenta.

Generously butter eight 5-ounce ramekins. Line the bottom with a circle of parchment. Butter the parchment. Distribute the custard among the ramekins. Place the ramekins on a baking sheet and bake until set, 20 to 25 minutes. Remove from the oven and run a small knife around the edges. Let sit for 5 minutes. Invert the custards onto individual serving plates.

To serve, warm the stewed fruit and spoon some of the fruit and sauce around the custards. Drizzle with crème fraîche. Dust with confectioners' sugar.

SERVES 8

ITALY BY CANDLELIGHT

Here is a menu for an elegant evening at home with friends.

Bagna Cauda, a Warm Italian Bath (page 58)
Prosciutto, Parmigiano, and Pepper Breadsticks (page 60)
Golden-Sautéed Veal with Arugula and Tomato Salad (page 242)
Warm Polenta Custards with Grappa-Soaked Golden Raisins
    (page 259)

Caramel Pot de Crème

I like anything with butterscotch, even butterscotch Lifesavers! When I was growing up, I think we were the only kids on the block who had dessert every night. The flavor of this caramel *pot de crème* is reminiscent of the gooey butterscotch pudding my mom often made for us. It's a perfect autumn dessert served with Maple Leaf Cookies (page 290). You can make these rich custards several hours ahead and store them in the refrigerator. Just remember to bring them to room temperature before serving; they will taste best this way. (This goes for practically everything but ice cream! When dishes are too cold—or too hot for that matter—the extreme temperature can mask much of the flavor.)

1 cup granulated sugar
⅓ plus ¼ cup water
2½ cups heavy cream
1½ cups milk
8 egg yolks
Boiling water for the pan
1 tablespoon confectioners' sugar

Place the granulated sugar and ⅓ cup water in a large, deep, heavy saucepan over medium-high heat. Cover and bring to a boil. Boil for 2 to 3 minutes. Remove the cover and cook, swirling the pan, until the sugar turns a golden amber color, 8 to 12 minutes. Be very careful, the caramel is very hot.

Meanwhile, place 1½ cups of the cream and the milk in a large saucepan over medium-high heat. Cook until it bubbles around the edges. Turn off the heat.

Preheat the oven to 325°F.

When the caramel is ready, carefully add the remaining ¼ cup water and whisk vigorously until the bubbles subside. Pour the caramel into the warm cream and whisk together until mixed. Let cool for 10 minutes.

In a bowl, whisk together the egg yolks. With a wooden spoon, slowly add the caramel mixture to the egg yolks, stirring constantly until mixed. Strain through a fine-mesh strainer into a bowl.

Pour the custard into six 6-ounce ramekins. Place the ramekins in a baking pan and fill the pan with boiling water to come 1 inch up the sides of the ramekins. Bake until the edges are firm and the very centers are still slightly jiggly, 40 to 50 minutes. Remove from the oven and let sit in the water bath for 10 minutes. Remove from the water bath and let cool at room temperature for 30 minutes. Refrigerate for several hours or overnight until cold.

Just before serving, whip the remaining 1 cup cream to soft peaks. Stir in the confectioners' sugar.

To serve, top each *pot de crème* with a dollop of whipped cream and serve directly from the ramekins at room temperature.

SERVES 6

Caramelized Orange and Rice Custard

In the recipe for this delicious rice custard, I give you three different choices for the rice: vialone nano, carnaroli, and arborio. You may be familiar with only arborio, but like arborio, the other two types of rice are commonly grown in northern Italy and used to make risotto. Any of these rice varieties will yield a creamy grain with a bit of toothy texture that will be perfect for this custard. By the way, this dessert is excellent without the crème anglaise and caramel sauce, but if you have the time and want to make a more dramatic presentation, serve it with both. When making the caramel sauce, know that after you add the orange juice, it may take a few minutes to get to a slightly thickened consistency.

CARAMEL RICE CUSTARD

3 cups sugar

$\frac{1}{2}$ to $\frac{3}{4}$ cup fresh orange juice or blood orange juice

1 cup vialone nano, carnaroli, or arborio rice

3 cups milk

2 tablespoons unsalted butter

2 teaspoons finely grated orange zest

5 eggs

Boiling water for the pan

CRÈME ANGLAISE

1$\frac{1}{2}$ cups milk

3 egg yolks

3 tablespoons sugar

$\frac{1}{2}$ teaspoon vanilla extract

Make the caramel: Place 2 cups of the sugar in a large heavy stainless steel skillet over medium heat until it begins to melt. Do not use a spoon to stir the sugar, instead swirl the pan to melt the sugar uniformly. Cook until the sugar starts to turn golden brown or caramel color. Immediately remove the pan from the heat and pour half of the caramel into an 8-inch round cake pan. Turn the pan to coat the bottom and sides with caramel. Set aside. Immediately add the orange juice to the skillet and cook over medium heat, stirring, until the sauce is smooth again. Remove from the heat and let cool.

Preheat the oven to 400°F. Bring a large saucepan of water to a boil. Add the rice and simmer for 5 minutes. Drain. Rinse the saucepan, add the milk, and bring to a scald. Add the rice and cook, stirring occasionally, until done, 10 to 15 minutes. Remove from the heat. Add the remaining 1 cup sugar, the butter, and orange zest, and stir until dissolved. Place the eggs in a large bowl and beat them together. Add a quarter of the rice to the eggs and stir together. Continue until all of the rice has been added. Let stand for 5 minutes. Pour the egg-rice mixture into the caramel-lined cake pan. Set the pan in a larger baking pan with enough boiling water to reach halfway up the sides of the cake pan. Cover with aluminum foil. Bake in the middle of the oven until a skewer comes out clean, 50 to 60 minutes.

Make the crème anglaise: In a medium saucepan, scald the milk. Whisk the egg yolks and sugar together in another saucepan. Slowly whisk the scalded milk into the egg yolk mixture. Cook over medium-low heat, stirring constantly, until the mixture coats the back of a spoon and registers 170°F with an instant-read thermometer. Strain through a fine-mesh strainer into a bowl. Add the vanilla and set aside.

Remove the baking pan from the oven. Remove the custard from the water bath, run a knife around the edge of the custard and let stand for 10 minutes. Invert the custard onto a serving dish.

To serve, spoon some crème anglaise onto a serving plate. Top with a wedge of custard. Drizzle with the orange caramel sauce.

SERVES 8

Caramelized Chocolate Almond Budino

You're wondering what a *budino* is, right? *Budino* is the Italian word for "custard" or "pudding." This one is incredibly rich and creamy, filled with almonds, chocolate, and Amaretti cookie crumbs. Amaretti cookies are available at any well-stocked market. You've probably seen them, but didn't know what they were. Oftentimes they come in a brightly painted orange container. The cookies are wrapped individually in tissue paper and add a lot of flavor to this dessert!

1¾ cups sugar

4½ ounces bittersweet or semisweet chocolate, chopped

3 cups milk

8 eggs

1 cup ground amaretti cookies (5 ounces)

½ cup finely ground toasted almonds

3 tablespoons all-purpose flour

Boiling water for the pan

In a large heavy stainless steel frying pan over medium heat, melt 1 cup of the sugar. Do not use a spoon, instead swirl the pan to melt the sugar uniformly. Cook until the sugar starts to turn golden brown or caramel color. Immediately remove from the heat and pour the mixture into a 9-inch round cake pan. Turn the pan to coat the bottom and sides. Set aside.

In the top of a double boiler, melt the chocolate. In a large saucepan, scald the milk and add the chocolate, whisking constantly. Stir in the remaining ¾ cup sugar and remove from the heat. In a bowl, stir together the amaretti crumbs, almonds, and flour. Add to the chocolate mixture and whisk together until mixed.

Preheat the oven to 375°F. Pour the custard-mixture into the caramel lined pan and place in a larger baking pan. Pour in enough boiling water to come 1 inch up the sides of the cake pan. Bake in the oven until set, 65 to 75 minutes.

Remove the custard from the oven and let sit for 15 minutes. Invert the *budino* onto a serving plate.

SERVES 12 TO 16

CITY LIGHTS

I am a fanatic about lighting. Whether electrical or candle, the lighting has got to add to the atmosphere of warmth and intimacy I strive for in decorating. I prefer dim, but sufficient lighting, and low, preferably beeswax, candles in white or ivory—low to encourage conversation, and beeswax, as they don't impart a scent.

One of my favorite things is to put little tea lights into small, tinted Moroccan glasses, which then cast an amazing ambient light onto my table (and the tea lights last for hours). I also love to use the Majolica candlesticks that I brought back from Italy.

The thing about candles is that they set a mood more than just provide lighting. And the more intimate the occasion, the more candles I use.

Summer Fruits in Sweet Spiced Wine

My favorite desserts of all are fruit desserts, whether it's a sorbet, a fruit tart, or just a simple bowl of summer fruit. Don't get me wrong, I like a bite of good chocolate every once in a while. But in the summertime, I prefer summer stone fruit and berries of all kinds. In this dessert, I've combined them with a late harvest dessert wine for an easy, but really flavorful dessert when time is of the essence!

1 orange

1½ cups late harvest dessert wine (Riesling, Gewürztraminer, Muscat, Sauternes)

1 tablespoon honey

½ vanilla bean, split and scraped

4 ¼-inch slices fresh ginger root

1 pint blackberries

1½ cups green seedless grapes (about 8 ounces)

1 cup cherries, pitted (about 6 ounces)

2 nectarines, halved, pitted, and diced

2 plums, halved, pitted, and diced

Cut the peel from the orange with a vegetable peeler, making sure there is no white pith. Juice the orange. Bring the orange juice, orange peel, wine, honey, vanilla bean, and ginger to a boil in a saucepan over high heat. Reduce the heat to low and simmer for 5 minutes. Remove from the heat and discard the orange peel, vanilla bean, and ginger slices. Let cool for 30 minutes.

Meanwhile, place the blackberries, grapes, cherries, nectarines, and plums in a bowl. Pour the wine syrup over the fruit and refrigerate for 20 minutes to chill the fruit. Stir gently just until mixed.

To serve, spoon the fruit into bowls and pour the sauce over the top.

SERVES 6

Watermelon, Mango, Blueberries, and Lime "Salad"

I didn't really take a serious interest in cooking until I was in college. Still, I was always pretty aware of good ingredients. That's not surprising, since as a kid I watched my mother labor over the perfect bushel basket of peaches or worry over whether the wild blueberries on my grandfather's farm were ready to pick. (Though this really had more to do with who was going to get them first: us or the birds!) The one thing I knew for sure was that my mother loved everything fresh. This "salad" is a tribute to her and to that conviction about fresh ingredients!

> 3 tablespoons orange juice
>
> 1 tablespoon lime juice
>
> 2 teaspoons sugar
>
> 1 teaspoon lime zest
>
> 2$\frac{1}{2}$ pounds seedless watermelon, rind removed, cut into $\frac{3}{4}$-inch chunks
>
> 2 mangoes, peeled and diced into $\frac{1}{2}$-inch chunks
>
> 2 cups blueberries
>
> 6 mint leaves, cut into thin strips, as a garnish

Place the orange juice, lime juice, sugar, and lime zest in a large bowl and whisk together. Add the watermelon, mangoes, and blueberries and toss together. Refrigerate for 1 hour. Serve garnished with mint.

SERVES 6

Little Almond and Plum Galettes

A galette is just a rustic, free-form pie. I love to serve these little individual galettes hot from the oven with vanilla ice cream melting over the top. (They're also perfect for picnics.) But how do you serve them hot when company is coming and you don't want to get stuck in the kitchen? Assemble them several hours in advance and store the uncooked galettes in the refrigerator. When your guests arrive, pop them in the oven. Make sure the fruit you use is fairly firm or the filling will be too juicy and make the bottoms of the galettes soggy.

2½ cups all-purpose flour

3 tablespoons almond paste

2 sticks (½ pound) unsalted butter, cut into ½-inch dice and chilled in
    freezer for 1 hour

10 tablespoons sugar

Pinch of salt

¾ to 1 cup ice water

3 tablespoons ground almonds

1 pound plums, halved, pitted, and thinly sliced

Vanilla ice cream

Place the flour and almond paste in a food processor and pulse until well mixed. Place the mixture in the freezer for 1 hour.

Place the flour-almond paste mixture with the butter, 3 tablespoons of the sugar, and the salt in the food processor and pulse until half the mixture is the size of peas and the other half is like oatmeal. Turn out the mixture onto a work surface and make a well in the center. Add the ice water, a little at a time, just until the dough holds together.

Roll out the dough on a well-floured surface. Cut into 6 rounds, each about 6 to 7 inches in diameter. Place on rimmed baking sheets in a single layer.

Combine 3 tablespoons of the sugar and the almonds together in a bowl. Sprinkle 1 tablespoon of the mixture onto the center of each of the pastry rounds to within 1 inch of the edge. Refrigerate while you assemble the filling.

In a bowl, toss the plums together with the remaining 4 tablespoons sugar.

Preheat the oven to 375°F. Remove the pastry from the refrigerator. Spread the plums over the center of each round, distributing evenly and leaving a 1-inch border uncovered. Fold the uncovered edge of the pastry over the plums, pleating it to make it fit. Bake the galettes until golden brown, 20 to 25 minutes. Remove from the oven and let cool for 5 minutes. Slide the galettes off the pan and onto a serving plate.

Place each galette on a serving plate, scoop ice cream alongside, and serve.

SERVES 6

Dried Plum and Walnut Caramel Tart

A few years back, I worked with the California Dried Plum Council (the organization responsible for "changing" the name of prunes to dried plums). It was a wonderful project for me, because for years I have been known to pour myself a glass of prune juice, add prunes to my daily smoothie, and enjoy popping them in my mouth when I want a bite of something sweet, yet healthy. I have always enjoyed this tart when I made it jam-packed with walnuts, but then I added dried plums for a whole new dessert! Drizzling the top of the finished tart with threads of chocolate seems more difficult than it really is—and it makes the tart even more special.

> ³/₄ cup walnuts
> ³/₄ cup heavy cream
> ³/₄ cup sugar
> 1 tablespoon walnut oil
> 1 cup pitted and coarsely chopped dried plums
> 1 prebaked Short Crust Tart Shell (recipe follows)
> 2 ounces bittersweet chocolate, chopped

Preheat the oven to 375°F. Place the walnuts on a baking sheet and bake until they smell nutty and are light golden, 5 to 7 minutes. Increase the oven temperature to 400°F.

In a saucepan over medium-high heat, mix the cream, sugar, and walnut oil. Bring to a boil, reduce the heat, and boil gently until the mixture thickens slightly, about 3 minutes. Remove from the heat, add the walnuts and dried plums and stir together. Let stand for 15 minutes.

Pour the filling into the prebaked tart shell, distributing the nuts and dried plums evenly. Bake in the oven until the top is a combination of creamy white and russet caramel and looks like rice krispies, 30 to 40 minutes. Let the tart cool on a rack for 15 minutes. Loosen the pastry from the side of the pan with a thin paring knife.

Melt the chocolate in the top of a double boiler. With a fork, using a back and forth motion, drizzle threads of chocolate onto the top of the tart, distributing evenly. Cut the tart into squares and serve.

SERVES 8

Prebaked Short Crust Tart Shell

1¼ cups all-purpose flour

1 tablespoon sugar

Pinch of salt

10 tablespoons (5 ounces) butter, cut into 12 pieces and out of the
   refrigerator for 15 minutes

1 tablespoon cold water, or more if needed

In a food processor, mix the flour, sugar, and salt with a few pulses. Add the butter and pulse until the mixture resembles cornmeal. Add the water, or more as needed, until the pastry is blended and will hold together if you press it. Gather it into a ball, flatten it into a 6-inch disk, and wrap it in plastic wrap. Refrigerate it for 30 minutes.

Preheat the oven to 400°F. Press the pastry evenly into the bottom and 1 inch up the sides of a 9-inch round tart pan. Set the pastry-lined pan in the freezer for 30 minutes.

Line the pastry with parchment paper and scatter 1 cup of dried beans or pie weights onto the parchment. Bake the tart shell until the top edges are light golden, 10 to 15 minutes. Remove the parchment and weights, reduce the oven temperature to 375°F, and continue to bake until the pastry is light golden, 10 to 15 minutes.

Warm Chocolate, Cinnamon, and Coffee Tart

Years ago in Mexico City, I tasted a tart like this and have thought about it ever since. One of the New World foods, chocolate has always been a favorite in Mexico (and every-where else, for that matter), especially when it's paired with cinnamon and coffee. Try this combination of true Mexican flavors!

3/4 cup pine nuts

4 ounces bittersweet chocolate, chopped

3 tablespoons unsalted butter, cut into 8 pieces

2/3 cup dark corn syrup

2 tablespoons granulated sugar

2 tablespoons Kahlúa or brandy

2 1/2 teaspoons instant espresso powder

3/4 teaspoon cinnamon

3 eggs

1 prebaked Short Crust Tart Shell (page 275)

1 cup heavy cream

2 tablespoons confectioners' sugar

1/4 teaspoon vanilla extract

Preheat the oven to 350°F.

Place the pine nuts in a dry skillet and cook over medium heat, stirring, until golden, 1 to 2 minutes. Set aside to cool.

In a double boiler over medium-high heat, melt the chocolate and butter, stirring until smooth. In another saucepan over medium-high heat, stir together the corn syrup and granulated sugar until boiling. Add to the melted chocolate. In a small bowl, whisk together the Kahlúa, espresso powder, and cinnamon. Place the eggs in a large bowl and whisk until foamy. Add the Kahlúa mixture and whisk until well

mixed. Add the chocolate and whisk until well mixed. Stir in the toasted pine nuts. Pour the filling into the prebaked tart shell and bake until a skewer comes out of the center clean, 35 to 40 minutes. Let the tart cool for 15 to 20 minutes.

Meanwhile, whip the cream to soft peaks. Add 1 tablespoon of the confectioners' sugar and vanilla and stir together.

Cut the tart into wedges, dust the top with the remaining 1 tablespoon confectioners' sugar and serve with the soft cream.

SERVES 8 TO 10

> *"Venice is like eating an entire box of chocolate liqueurs at one go."*
>
> TRUMAN CAPOTE

Flakiest Apricot and Raspberry Tart

This tart is built on the simplest, no-excuses pastry. You can't go wrong or mess it up! Better still, it's free-form, so there's no tart pan to fight with. The finished tart has a wonderful rustic appearance and, with the fruit's intense colors and flavors, would be a great choice for a picnic. (Feel free to experiment with your own color and flavor combinations. Just be sure to select fruit at its peak ripeness.) I have a word of caution when you're assembling the dough: Make sure to freeze the butter and flour for an hour prior to making it. If, during the process of making the dough, the butter starts to soften and warms up, pop it in the freezer until ice cold again. The dough can be stored for up to three days or frozen for up to a month. Substitute peeled peaches, plums, or nectarines if apricots aren't available.

PASTRY

1 cup all-purpose flour

$^1/_3$ cup cake flour

2 tablespoons sugar

$^1/_8$ teaspoon salt

1$^1/_2$ sticks (6 ounces) unsalted
    butter, cut into $^1/_2$-inch pieces

$^1/_4$ cup ice water

2 teaspoon lemon juice

TOPPING

10 to 12 fresh medium-ripe
    apricots, halved, pitted, and cut
    into $^1/_2$-inch slices

3 tablespoons sugar

2 cups fresh raspberries

2 tablespoons butter, melted

$^1/_2$ cup apricot jam, melted and
    strained

Vanilla ice cream

Make the pastry: Mix the all-purpose flour, cake flour, sugar, and salt in a bowl. Place in the freezer for 1 hour before using. Place the butter in a bowl in the freezer for 1 hour before using.

In a food processor, pulse the ice-cold flour and butter several times, until half of the butter is the size of peas and the other half is smaller than peas. Pour the contents into a bowl. Combine the ice water and lemon juice and add to the flour mixture a little at a time just until the dough begins to hold together.

Turn the dough out onto a lightly floured work surface and press together as best you can to form a rough rectangle shape, about 4 inches x 6 inches. There will be large chunks of butter showing. Do not knead. Roll out the dough into a ½-inch-thick rectangle, 6 inches x 10 inches. Fold in the narrow ends to meet in the center. Fold in half again so that there are four layers. This is your first turn so that the folded edges are on your right and left. Repeat the whole process from the rolling point. This is your second turn. Turn the dough a quarter of a turn and roll again to form another 6 x 10 inch ½-inch-thick rectangle. This time, fold into thirds as you would a business letter. Wrap the dough in plastic wrap and refrigerate for 60 minutes.

Preheat the oven to 400°F.

Assemble the tart: Combine the apricots and sugar. Roll out the dough into a 12 x 13-inch square and trim to make an 11- to 12-inch round. Place on a baking sheet and crimp the edges. Place the apricots in an overlapping decorative pattern around the perimeter of the tart just inside the edge. Next, place 2 rows of raspberries hull side down. Place the remaining apricots in an overlapping decorative pattern in the center of the tart.

Brush the fruit with the melted butter and bake the tart in the middle of the oven for 10 minutes. Reduce the oven temperature to 375°F and continue to bake until golden and crisp, 25 to 35 minutes. Remove the tart from the oven and brush with the jam. Let cool for 10 minutes.

To serve, cut into wedges and place a scoop of ice cream alongside.

SERVES 6 TO 8

Plum Cake

My family is really into food: While we're eating one meal, we're planning the next. I'd say we are probably obsessed with cooking and eating. Of course, it's all my mother's fault. She comes from a long line of chefs and cooks and, take it from me, she loves the kitchen and anything to do with food. She called me one day: "I made the most amazing plum cake—you need to put it in your next book." This means that she probably made it twelve times. She'll make a recipe constantly until she's tired of it, perfected it, or the fruit or vegetable has gone out of season. But this was the first time she insisted I put one of her recipes in my book, so I decided to test the recipe. Aren't our mothers always right? By the way, this dessert would be equally good for dessert or afternoon tea . . . while you're discussing your next meal!

½ cup unsalted butter, at room temperature
⅔ cup plus 1 teaspoon granulated sugar
2 eggs, at room temperature
1 tablespoon grated lemon zest
1 teaspoon vanilla extract
1 cup all-purpose flour
1 teaspoon baking powder
½ teaspoon salt
6 small, firm, ripe plums, pitted and halved
¼ teaspoon cinnamon
Confectioners' sugar

Preheat the oven to 350°F. Using an electric mixer, cream the butter and ⅔ cup of the granulated sugar until light and creamy, about 2 minutes. Add the eggs, one at a time, beating well after each addition. Add the lemon zest and vanilla and beat for 2 more minutes.

Butter an 8-inch round cake pan. Dust with flour and tap out the excess. In a bowl, sift together the flour, baking powder, and salt. Add the dry ingredients to the creamed mixture and beat just until combined. Spoon the batter into the prepared pan. Place the plum halves skin side up on top of the batter.

In a small bowl, stir together the cinnamon and remaining 1 teaspoon sugar. Sprinkle over the plums. Bake until the sides of the cake come away from the pan, 35 to 40 minutes. Remove from the oven and run a small knife around the edge of the pan. Let the cake cool for 20 minutes on a cooling rack.

Cover the cake with a plate and flip over to turn it out. Invert the cake onto a serving plate so that the plums are on top. While the cake is still hot, dust the top with confectioners' sugar.

SERVES 6 TO 8

Cranberry Upside-Down Cake

I continue to be influenced by Chez Panisse, where I cooked for several years. This recipe was inspired by Lindsey Shere, who was the pastry chef when I worked there. There is something I love about her style, simplicity mixed with assertive flavors. And I love how this dessert looks: a beautiful white cake crowned with red berries. Whenever the weather gets cold, Thanksgiving approaches, or I see a bag of cranberries at the store, I can't help but think about Lindsey and this beautiful cake.

1½ sticks (6 ounces) unsalted
   butter
¾ cup packed light brown sugar
¾ pound cranberries
1½ cups flour
2 teaspoons baking powder
¼ teaspoon salt
1 cup granulated sugar

2 egg yolks
1 teaspoon plus a few drops vanilla
   extract
½ cup milk
2 egg whites
¼ teaspoon cream of tartar
1 cup heavy cream
1 tablespoon confectioners' sugar

Place 4 tablespoons of the butter and the brown sugar in a 9-inch cake pan over medium heat, stirring until the sugar is melted, 1 minute. Swirl to coat the sides with the butter. Place the cranberries on top of the melted butter and sugar.

Preheat the oven to 350°F. In a bowl, toss together the flour, baking powder, and salt. Cream the remaining 8 tablespoons butter and the sugar together in another bowl. Add the egg yolks to the creamed mixture, 1 at a time, beating well after each addition. Add 1 teaspoon of the vanilla and mix well. Add the milk alternately with the dry ingredients, folding well after each addition.

Beat the egg whites to soft peaks. Add the cream of tartar and continue to beat until the peaks hold their shape. Fold the whites into the cake batter. Spread the batter over the fruit in the cake pan and bake until a toothpick inserted into the center of the cake comes out clean, 55 to 60 minutes.

Remove the cake from the oven and run a small knife around the edge of the pan. Let the cake cool for 15 minutes. Invert the cake onto a serving platter and let it sit for another 5 minutes with the pan on the top. Remove the pan.

Whip the cream to soft peaks. Add a few drops of vanilla and the confectioners' sugar and mix.

Serve slices of cake with the softly whipped cream.

SERVES 8 TO 10

> *"Everything about Florence seems to be colored with a mild violet, like diluted wine."*
>
> HENRY JAMES

Triple Ginger Pineapple Cake

I didn't want to call this cake a pineapple upside-down cake for fear that you would immediately conjure up images of dry cake crowned with canned pineapple rings targeted in the center with maraschino cherries. This cake is a far cry from the traditional version. I just love it! And the funny thing is, if you asked any of my friends if I have a sweet tooth, they would say pretty sternly "No!" But when it comes to this cake, I never refuse a slice. If you love ginger and pineapple like I do, and you get them together in a moist cake, you won't refuse a slice either! Serve with softly whipped cream or vanilla ice cream.

TOPPING

4 tablespoons butter

1/3 cup packed brown sugar

2 1/2 cups diced fresh pineapple

3 tablespoons diced crystallized
    ginger

CAKE

1 1/2 cups flour

3 teaspoons ground ginger

2 teaspoons baking powder

1/4 teaspoon salt

1 stick (4 ounces) butter

3/4 cup sugar

2 tablespoons grated fresh ginger

2 egg yolks

1 teaspoon vanilla extract

1/2 cup milk

2 egg whites

Make the topping: Butter a 9-inch round nonstick cake pan. Melt the butter and brown sugar in the bottom of the cake pan. Combine the pineapple and crystallized ginger in a bowl and place the mixture on top of the melted butter and sugar in an even layer.

Make the cake: Preheat the oven to 350°F. Mix the flour, ginger, baking powder, and salt together. Cream the butter, sugar, and grated fresh ginger together in a bowl until light, about 2 minutes. Add the egg yolks one at a time, beating well after each addition. Add the vanilla and mix well. Using a large rubber spatula, stir in the milk alternately with the dry ingredients, folding well after each addition.

Beat the egg whites until stiff and the peaks hold their shape. Fold the whites into the cake batter. Spread the batter over the fruit and bake until a toothpick inserted into the center of the cake comes out clean, 40 to 50 minutes.

Remove from the oven and let sit for 10 minutes. Run a small knife around the edge of the pan. Place a large serving plate on top and invert the cake onto the plate.

SERVES 10 TO 12

FRESH FRUIT CRISP IN A FLASH

When I make a fresh fruit crisp, I double or triple the topping and freeze it. When I need a quick dessert, I cut up 8 cups of fresh fruit in season, toss with 2 tablespoons of sugar and 3 tablespoons of all-purpose flour, place in a 2- to 2½-quart baking dish, and top with the frozen topping. I bake it for 35 to 40 minutes at 375°F and serve it with lots of vanilla ice cream.

FOR THE CRISP TOPPING

¾ cup pecans or walnuts, toasted

1½ cups all-purpose flour

½ cup brown sugar

¼ teaspoon freshly grated nutmeg

1 stick (4 ounces) unsalted butter, at room temperature

Place the nuts in a food processor and pulse a few times until they are ¼ inch in size. Reserve. In a bowl, mix the flour, brown sugar, and nutmeg. Add the dry ingredients and butter to the food processor and pulse until it just begins to hold together. Add the nuts and pulse 3 to 4 more times until mixed.

Walnut Torte with Maple Cream

Madeleine Kamman is a brilliant French cooking teacher; she has and will continue to inspire me for years and years. I first studied with her while I was living in Boston in 1976. Then in 1985, I studied with her for a whole year both in France and the United States. She has always loved the mountains, and New England continues to be a place that she returns to again and again. This moist, rich torte recipe, redolent of walnuts and maple, was conceived during her years living there. It would be a wonderful dessert to serve your guests in the fall and winter months. I have adapted this recipe from her book *The Making of a Cook*. Madeleine, thanks for your continued inspiration.

> 2 cups walnut halves
>
> 2/3 cup plus 2 tablespoons finely ground vanilla-wafer crumbs
>
> 6 eggs, separated
>
> 2/3 cup sugar
>
> 1 teaspoon instant espresso powder
>
> 1/2 teaspoon maple flavoring
>
> Pinch of salt
>
> 3/4 cup walnut halves
>
> 1 1/2 cups heavy cream
>
> 3 tablespoons maple syrup

In a food processor, grind the walnuts with 2/3 cup vanilla wafer crumbs until finely ground. Reserve. Butter two 8-inch round cake pans. Line the bottom with parchment paper and butter the parchment. Dust with the remaining 2 tablespoons vanilla-wafer crumbs. Tap out the excess.

Preheat the oven to 350°F. Place the egg yolks, sugar, espresso powder, 1/4 teaspoon of the maple flavoring, and the salt in a bowl. Using an electric mixer, beat until very light in color and creamy. In a separate bowl, beat the egg whites to stiff peaks. Immediately fold one-quarter of the egg whites into the egg yolk mixture to lighten the mixture. Fold the remaining egg whites into the yolk mixture. Sprinkle the ground walnut mixture onto the top of the batter. Fold together just until mixed. Divide the batter between the two prepared pans.

Bake the tortes until a skewer inserted into the center comes out clean, 20 to 25 minutes. Let the cakes cool on cooling racks. When the cakes are cool, using a serrated knife, split the tortes across into 2 rounds.

Preheat the oven to 375°F. Place the walnut halves on a baking sheet and bake until light golden and hot to the touch, 5 to 7 minutes. Chop the walnuts.

Whip the heavy cream to soft peaks. Add the remaining ¼ teaspoon maple flavoring and the maple syrup. Spread the cream between the 4 layers and on the top and side of the torte. Sprinkle the top of the torte with the chopped walnuts. Refrigerate the cake for at least 1 and up to 3 hours, but remove it from the refrigerator 10 minutes before serving.

SERVES 8

Maple Leaf Cookies

These cookies are inspired by the changing colors of the maple leaves during the fall, one of the purest pleasures of my New England childhood. The dough can be made several days ahead and stored in the refrigerator until ready to bake. Serve them with Caramel Pot de Crème (page 261).

2 sticks (½ pound) unsalted butter, at room temperature

¾ cup sugar, plus more for sprinkling

½ cup pure maple syrup

1 teaspoon vanilla extract

1 egg yolk

3 cups all-purpose flour

¼ teaspoon salt

Using an electric mixer, cream the butter and sugar together until light and fluffy, about 3 minutes. Add the maple syrup, vanilla, and egg yolk and mix well for 1 minute. Sift the flour and salt on top of the mixture and mix until well combined. Wrap the dough in plastic wrap and refrigerate overnight.

Preheat the oven to 350°F.

Divide the dough into 2 pieces. Working with 1 piece at a time, roll out the dough ⅛ inch thick on a lightly floured surface. With a maple leaf cookie cutter, 4 inches across the widest part, cut as many cookies as possible. As they are cut, place them 1 inch apart on a lightly buttered baking sheet. With a small paring knife, mark the cookies to resemble the veins of a maple leaf. Roll the remaining scraps and cut additional cookies. Repeat with the other half of the dough. Sprinkle each cookie with about ½ teaspoon sugar.

Bake the cookies until the edges are lightly golden, 10 to 12 minutes. Let cool on a rack.

MAKES 2 TO 2½ DOZEN

Ginger Crisps

I remember the first time I worked with Dan Yamamoto in San Francisco. He was not only one of my most efficient assistants, he also gave me a memorable gift: these cookies. Now I get to present them to you! For a treat, serve with an Italian Lemon "Milkshake" (page 293).

¼ cup unblanched almonds	⅔ cup sugar
1½ cups all-purpose flour	1 egg
½ teaspoon baking powder	½ teaspoon vanilla extract
¼ teaspoon ground ginger	⅔ cup chopped crystallized ginger
Pinch of salt	
1 stick (4 ounces) unsalted butter, at room temperature	

Preheat the oven to 350°F. Bring a saucepan of water to a boil. Add the almonds and boil for 20 seconds. Drain the almonds and let cool. With your fingernail, break the skin of the almonds and pop them out of the skins. Place the almonds on a baking sheet and bake until light golden, 6 to 8 minutes. Let cool for 10 minutes. Place the almonds in a food processor with the flour, baking powder, ginger, and salt and process until pulverized. Set aside.

Using an electric mixer, cream the butter and sugar together until pale in color. Add the egg and vanilla and beat until well mixed. Gradually add the flour mixture to the creamed mixture until well mixed. Stir in the crystallized ginger. Transfer the dough to a work surface, and using the side of a ruler or spatula, form the dough into a rectangular log, about 1½ x 2½ x 8 inches. Wrap well in plastic wrap and freeze until firm, about 1 hour or overnight.

While still frozen, slice the dough into ⅛-inch-thick slices and place on ungreased baking sheets. Bake until light golden around the edges, about 10 minutes. Remove from the pan and place on a cooling rack. Let cool completely.

MAKES 4 TO 5 DOZEN

Italian Lemon "Milkshake"

This is no ordinary milkshake (not one for kids, either)! Called *sgropino* in Italy, it's the most deceptively innocent thing you'll ever drink. Spiked with plenty of vodka and Prosecco, a naturally sparkling wine from Italy, it packs a real punch. Serve this in a sexy, little, frosted martini, wine, or champagne glass along with Ginger Crisps (page 291) or biscotti in lieu of dessert after a big dinner. Icy cold, it is refreshing in both summer and winter!

2 cups vanilla ice cream
1¹/₂ cups lemon sorbet
³/₄ cups fresh lemon juice
²/₃ cup vodka
¹/₂ cup Prosecco

Place all of the ingredients in a blender and process until thick and creamy. Pour into glasses and serve immediately.

SERVES 8

THE "OTHER" BUBBLY

Champagne is the best-known sparkling wine, but equally delightful is the Italian sparkling wine Prosecco, named for the grape of the same name and grown in the Veneto in northeastern Italy. With its own, unique taste and appeal, Prosecco is crisp, appley, dry, and easier to drink (with less alcohol) and less expensive than champagne. You'll also like it in Bellinis (page 315).

Miss Judy's Sienese Almond Cookies

My dear friend Judy Witts Franchini, an expatriate living in Florence for the last twenty years, lives and cooks from her heart. She gave me this recipe for one of her favorite cookies from one of my favorite Italian cities, Siena. She says that the diamond shape is supposed to resemble the eyes of a Renaissance Madonna. To this day in Siena, every home will serve these cookies at Christmastime. (If you want to serve them in your home during the holidays, make them ahead and store them in an airtight container for several weeks.)

2 cups blanched almonds

1 cup sugar

1 cup plus 2 tablespoons confectioners' sugar, plus more for dusting

1 teaspoon almond extract

2 egg whites

Preheat the oven to 350°F. Place the almonds on a baking sheet and toast until light golden, about 5 minutes. Remove and let cool.

Reduce the oven temperature to 325°F. Place the almonds and sugar in a food processor and pulse until finely ground. Add 1 cup of the confectioners' sugar, the almond extract, and the egg whites and pulse again.

Lightly dust a work surface with the remaining 2 tablespoons confectioners' sugar. Remove the dough from the mixer and divide into 2 pieces. Pat 1 piece into a 5 x 7-inch rectangle. Cut into diamond shapes using a 2-inch cookie cutter. Repeat with the second piece of dough. Place the cookies on a parchment-lined baking sheet and bake until dry but still a little soft in the center, 12 to 15 minutes. Let cool completely and then dust with confectioners' sugar.

MAKES 24 COOKIES

Chocolate Hazelnut Biscotti

Biscotti have been the rage for years. Whether you like to dip them into a cup of espresso, *vin santo,* or serve them alongside a bowl of gelati, they have a great crunchy texture. They get their name from the process by which they're cooked: biscotti means "twice cooked." The cookie is baked the first time in a log shape; then it's sliced and baked a second time until dry and crunchy. Though biscotti seem like a lot of work, they are actually pretty simple. And the best part is: You can make them weeks ahead and store them in an airtight container so you'll always have handmade goodies on hand when friends drop by! Hazelnuts can be purchased peeled, which will save you much time.

1 cup hazelnuts	1/3 cup unsweetened cocoa powder
1 stick (4 ounces) unsalted butter	1 teaspoon baking powder
1 cup sugar	1/2 teaspoon baking soda
2 whole eggs plus 1 egg yolk	1/4 teaspoon salt
1 tablespoon rum	5 ounces excellent-quality
2 3/4 cups all-purpose flour	bittersweet chocolate, chopped

Preheat the oven to 350°F. Place the hazelnuts on a baking sheet and bake until golden brown and fragrant, 10 to 12 minutes. Allow the hazelnuts to cool for 2 minutes and then rub them briskly in a rough kitchen towel to remove as much of the skin as possible. Chop the hazelnuts into 1/4-inch pieces and set aside.

Using an electric mixer, cream the butter and sugar together until light and fluffy. Add the eggs and yolk, 1 at a time, beating well after each addition. Add the rum and mix well. Sift together the flour, cocoa powder, baking powder, baking soda, and salt. Add the flour in thirds, folding in the last third by hand with the chocolate. Add the hazelnuts and mix well. Refrigerate the dough for 1 hour.

Divide the dough into 2 pieces and roll each piece into a sausage-like shape about 10 inches long. Place them on a parchment-lined baking. Flatten each sausage-like shape until it is 1 1/2 inches wide. Bake until a toothpick inserted into the center comes out clean, about 30 minutes. Let rest for 10 minutes. While the biscotti are warm, slice with a serrated knife, on a sharp diagonal, into ¹/₂-inch slices.

Reduce the oven temperature to 300°F. Place the biscotti cut side down on parchment-lined baking sheets and bake for 10 minutes. Turn the biscotti over and continue to bake until dry, about 10 minutes.

MAKES ABOUT 3 DOZEN

VIN SANTO

This wonderful sweet wine from Italy, pronounced "veen sahn-toh," means "holy wine" because it is heavenly to drink. It has a taste all its own, something like nuts and caramel, and a deep golden color.

The grapes for *vin santo* are harvested later in the year than grapes for table wine to give them more time to build up sugars, which also become more concentrated as the grapes begin to dry out on the vine. Once harvested, grapes are further dehydrated and then the must, or grape juice, is fermented and aged in oak or chestnut barrels for three to five years, and the wine exposed to cold winter temperatures and hot summers. This produces a great wine that is usually served as a dessert wine, although there are some *vin santo* that are drier and more suited to being drunk as an aperitif.

Apricot, Meyer Lemon, and Cardamom Triangles

Piping hot phyllo triangles filled with spicy apricots can be the perfect ending to the perfect meal, especially when they are scented with Meyer lemons. Meyer lemons are a sweet, shiny, smooth-skinned lemon that are great in desserts. In the past, they weren't readily available, but can now be found much more easily, especially during the winter months. If you can't find them, use Eureka or Lisbon lemons, the regular grocery store variety. You can fold the triangles ahead of time, store them in the refrigerator, and bake them at the last minute, if desired.

1¼ cups dried apricots (about 6 ounces)

2 tablespoons honey

1 tablespoon grated Meyer lemon zest or regular lemon zest

1 tablespoons Meyer lemon juice or regular lemon juice

2 teaspoons ground cardamom

½ pound phyllo dough (about 10 sheets)

1 stick (4 ounces) unsalted butter, melted

2 tablespoons sugar

Vanilla ice cream

Place the apricots in a saucepan and cover with water. Bring to a boil over high heat, reduce the heat to low, and simmer until the apricots are soft, 10 to 15 minutes. Drain the apricots and chop them. Place in a bowl with the honey, lemon zest, lemon juice, and cardamom. Stir together.

Preheat the oven to 400°F.

Place the phyllo to the side of your work surface and cover with a barely dampened kitchen towel. Place 1 sheet of phyllo on the work surface, brush lightly with melted butter and sprinkle lightly with sugar. Top with another sheet of phyllo. Brush lightly with butter and sprinkle lightly with sugar. Repeat until you have used all the phyllo, brushing the top sheet with butter. Cut the phyllo lengthwise into 3 separate strips, each one 4 x 18 inches. Cut the 3 strips in half crosswise into 6 pieces, each one 4 x 9 inches. Spoon one-sixth of the apricot mixture onto the end of 1 strip. Fold the corner over the filling to form a triangle. Continue to fold the entire strip as you would a flag. Repeat the whole process with the remaining phyllo strips until you have made 6 triangles. Place them on a buttered baking sheet and brush the top of the triangles with butter. Bake until golden brown, 15 to 20 minutes.

Place one of the triangles on a plate. Top with ice cream and serve immediately. (Note: If the triangles have cooled, you can reheat them in a 400°F. Bake the triangles on the top shelf of the oven until hot, 8 to 10 minutes.)

MAKES 6

Crispy Moroccan Phyllo with Orange Custard and Almonds

Like everything in Morocco, this dessert strikes a note of the truly exotic. I first tasted it on a visit to Marrakech years ago. There's something about the perfume of the orange flower water mixed with toasted almonds that compels me to have one bite after another. Don't think this dessert can only be served as the follow-up for a Moroccan meal; it is delicious as the conclusion to any dinner.

16 sheets phyllo dough

Vegetable oil for frying

1 cup blanched almonds

2 tablespoons confectioners' sugar

1½ teaspoons cinnamon

4 cups milk

4 tablespoons cornstarch

½ cup sugar

Pinch of salt

2 tablespoons ground blanched almonds

4 tablespoons orange-flower water

Using the bottom of a 9-inch round cake pan as a template, cut sixteen 9-inch rounds from the phyllo. Cover with a barely dampened kitchen towel.

Heat ½ inch of oil in a large skillet over medium-high heat. Press 2 pieces of phyllo together gently and place carefully in the oil; fry together until pale golden and crisp, 30 to 60 seconds. Drain on paper towels.

After you have fried all of the pieces of phyllo, brown the blanched almonds in the same oil until light golden, 30 to 60 seconds. Remove with a slotted spoon and drain on paper towels. When the almonds are cool, finely chop them. Place them in a bowl with the confectioners' sugar and cinnamon and toss together. Reserve.

In a small bowl, whisk together ¼ cup of the milk and the cornstarch. Place the remaining 3¾ cups milk and sugar in a saucepan until bubbles form around the edges. Stirring constantly with a wooden spoon, add the cornstarch mixture and cook until the sauce is thick and coats the spoon, 2 to 3 minutes. Add the ground almonds and orange-flower water. Whisk until smooth, about 1 minute. Remove from the heat and let the mixture cool.

Just before serving, place 2 sets of fried phyllo on top of one another on a large serving platter. Sprinkle with one third of the chopped almonds. Top with 2 sets of phyllo and dollop 2 spoonfuls of the almond custard sauce on top. With the back of a large spoon, press down on the leaves until you hear the phyllo crackle slightly. Top with 2 more sets of phyllo and sprinkle with one third of the almonds. Top with the remaining phyllo and dollop 2 spoonfuls of the custard sauce on top. With the back of a large spoon, press down on the leaves again until you hear the phyllo crackle slightly. Sprinkle with the remaining third of the almonds. Serve the remaining custard sauce in a small bowl.

SERVES 6 TO 8

"No city invites the heart to come to life as San Francisco does."

WILLIAM SAROYAN

Nectarine Sorbet with Blueberry Compote

The contrast of the cool, sunset-colored sorbet and deep blue compote makes this dessert as appealing to look at as it is delicious and refreshing to eat!

3 1/2 pounds nectarines

1 tablespoon plus 1 teaspoon lemon juice

1 1/3 cups sugar, or more or less as needed

3 1/2 cups blueberries

1/2 cup water

1 2-inch piece lemon zest

1 tablespoon crème de cassis

Drop the nectarines into boiling water for 30 seconds. With a slotted spoon, transfer the nectarines to a bowl of ice water. Peel and cut the nectarines coarsely. Discard the peels and all but 3 of the pits. Crack the three pits with a hammer or nutcracker and extract the kernels. Place the nectarines and kernels in a saucepan with 1 table-spoon of the lemon juice, and bring to a simmer over medium-high heat. Lower the heat to medium-low and simmer gently for 5 minutes. Remove from the heat. Put the nectarines in a blender and puree until very smooth.

While the mixture is still hot, strain through a fine-mesh strainer into a measuring cup. For each 4 cups of nectarine puree, you will need 1 cup of sugar. In a large bowl, combine the puree and add the correct amount of sugar and stir until the sugar is dissolved. Rub a little of the nectarine puree between your fingers to make sure that the sugar is melted and you can no longer feel any graininess. Place the mixture in the refrigerator and let cool completely. This can be done a day in advance.

Meanwhile, puree 1 cup of the blueberries in a food processor or blender until smooth. Strain through a fine-mesh strainer into a clean bowl. Place the water, the remaining ⅓ cup sugar, and the lemon zest in a medium pan over medium-high heat and bring to a boil. Reduce the heat to medium and add the remaining 2½ cups blueberries. Cook until the blueberries just begin to crack, about 30 seconds. Discard the lemon zest. Stir in the blueberry puree, crème de Cassis, and remaining 1 teaspoon lemon juice.

When the nectarine puree is well chilled, pour the mixture into an ice cream maker and freeze according to the manufacturer's instructions. Store in a covered container in the freezer.

To serve, warm the compote. Scoop the nectarine sorbet into bowls and spoon the compote over the top. Serve immediately.

MAKES APPROXIMATELY 1 QUART SORBET AND 2 CUPS COMPOTE

SORBET, SORBETTO, SHERBET

I make all kinds of fruit sorbet depending upon the season. The basic recipe is easily mastered. Once you know the fruit to sugar ratio, you can make sorbet with just about any fruit or fruit juice.

BASIC RECIPE

For each 4 cups fruit puree (watermelon, strawberry, mango, or pineapple, for example), add 1 cup sugar. For each 4 cups fruit juice (lemon, lime, grapefruit, or orange), add ¾ cup sugar and ¼ cup light corn syrup. Fruit like nectarines, peaches, or pears must be peeled and then stewed for a few minutes or the sorbet will oxidize and turn brown.

To melt the sugar, heat about ¼ of the puree or juice with the correct amount of sugar in a pan over medium heat and stir until the sugar is dissolved. If you are using fruit puree, rub a bit between your fingers to make sure the sugar is melted and you no longer feel any graininess. Place the mixture in the refrigerator and let cool completely. This can be done a day in advance.

When this mixture is well chilled, freeze according to the instructions on your ice cream maker.

Rose Petal Sorbet

If you are a rose gardener, or perhaps have a special admirer who gives you lots of fragrant, unsprayed roses, this is one of the most romantic desserts you can make. I prefer to use red roses so the sorbet has some color, but any color rose will do. To serve, scoop the rose petal sorbet into an unusual serving glass, perhaps a martini glass or a champagne flute, and garnish with a rose petal. Bring the glasses to the table and pour the champagne directly over the sorbet. It is inspired by my dear friend and chef Janni Kyritsis of Sydney, Australia.

> 1 cup sugar
> 1 cup water
> Rose petals from 6 unsprayed, large, strongly perfumed red roses
> 1 bottle champagne or sparkling wine

Place the sugar, water, and rose petals in a saucepan and bring to a boil over high heat. Remove the syrup from the heat and pour into a bowl. Refrigerate overnight.

The next day, strain and squeeze as much syrup out of the rose petals as possible. Measure the rose syrup. For each cup of rose syrup, add 2 cups champagne and stir together. Refrigerate the remaining champagne. Pour the mixture into an ice cream maker and freeze according to the manufacturer's instructions.

To serve, scoop the rose petal sorbet into glasses and pour a generous dash of the remaining champagne over the sorbet at the table.

SERVES 6

TABLE FOR TWO

When I'm giving a romantic dinner for two, I like to send a beautiful invitation (do this even if you've been together for twenty years). Get a very special bottle of wine. Set a small table in front of the fireplace, in a picture window, or in an area that's a little more intimate than your dining room. Use lots of candles. Start with a glass of champagne. And serve:

Oysters with Champagne Mignonette (page 90)
Truffle-Scented Roasted Cornish Hens with Prosciutto and Wild
   Mushrooms (page 182)
Rose Petal Sorbet (page 305)

or

Champagne Oyster Soup with Celery and Fennel (page 147)
Roulade of Herbed Lamb with Stewed Garlic (page 235)
Olive Oil–Mashed Potatoes (page 238)
Minted Sugar Snap Peas (page 238)
Double Chocolate Ice Cream with Dried Cherries (page 308)

Pear Granita

Italian "slush," that's what I call it! But to be honest, granita is a little bit more sophisticated than that. It isn't that it takes a lot of work or even special equipment (just periodic "forking" over a couple hours), but the flavor and pleasure of eating this simple dessert make it very special. The best part is that you can use pretty much any fruit in season: peaches, cherries, pineapple, lemons, watermelon, or mango. It has no fat whatsoever. Now is that a perfect dessert, or what?

> 6 peeled and cored Comice or Bartlett pears, cut into chunks
> (about 3 pounds)
> 1 cup water
> 1 cup sugar
> 1 tablespoon lemon juice

Place the pears in a pan with the water and sugar and simmer for 3 minutes. In a blender, puree the pear mixture until smooth. Stain through a fine mesh strainer. Add the lemon juice to the pear puree. Pour the mixture into a shallow 13 x 9-inch metal or glass baking dish and freeze until ice crystals begin to form, $1\frac{1}{2}$ to 2 hours. Whisk with a fork to move the crystals. Continue to whisk with a fork every 30 minutes for 2 hours until the mixture is completely crystallized and resembles slush.

Spoon or scoop the granita into ice-cold serving dishes. Serve immediately.

SERVES 6

Double Chocolate Ice Cream with Dried Cherries

I tend to think of myself as a pretty sensible, chocolate-by-itself kind of person. No raspberries and chocolate or orange and chocolate for me. Oh, I guess I could be tempted by mint and chocolate, especially the kind you find on your pillow when you return to your hotel with the turn-down-your-top-sheet service. And then there's cherries and chocolate. There's nothing better than chocolate-covered cherries, is there? I guess when it comes to chocolate, I lose all sense! This dessert — inspired by chocolate-covered cherries — is dedicated to pure pleasure; serve it as the culmination to a grand and lusty meal. (The cherry-flavored liqueur, maraschino, that this recipe calls for is from Italy; if it's unavailable, omit it from the ice cream and use port instead in the warm compote.)

2 cups heavy cream

2 cups milk

²/₃ cup sugar

10 ounces bittersweet chocolate, finely chopped

9 egg yolks

¹/₂ cup plus 3 tablespoons maraschino liqueur

10 ounces dried cherries

Place the heavy cream, milk, and sugar in a saucepan over medium heat. Heat until bubbles form around the edges of the pan.

Place 7 ounces of the chocolate in a large bowl and set a fine mesh strainer on top. Set aside.

In another saucepan, whisk the egg yolks. Add the scalded cream mixture to the egg yolks very slowly, whisking constantly. When all of it has been added, set the saucepan over medium heat and, *stirring constantly* with a flat-bottomed wooden spoon, cook until the mixture just coats the back of the spoon or until an instant-read thermometer registers 165°F. Immediately remove the pan from the heat and pour the custard through the strainer into the bowl of chocolate. Immediately whisk the custard and chocolate to melt the chocolate and cool the mixture. Add 3 tablespoons of the maraschino liqueur and refrigerate until cool.

Meanwhile, place 5 ounces of the dried cherries and the remaining ½ cup maraschino liqueur in a large saucepan. Heat over medium heat just until it bubbles around the edges. Remove from the heat and let stand for 30 minutes.

Pour the chilled ice cream base into an ice cream maker and freeze according to the manufacturer's instructions. During the churning process, 1 minute before the ice cream is done, add the remaining 3 ounces chopped chocolate and the remaining 5 ounces dried cherries.

To serve, reheat the maraschino syrup just until it bubbles around the edges. Scoop the ice cream into bowls. Spoon the dried cherries and maraschino syrup over the top. Serve immediately.

MAKES 1½ QUARTS ICE CREAM AND 1¼ CUPS SYRUP

INVITE THE KIDS

The great thing about ice cream is that it takes minutes to make and can be made completely ahead of time. It really is so simple. Think of it as nothing more than three ingredients: milk or cream, sugar, and egg yolks.

The hardest part might be selecting an ice cream maker. There are many choices, from very expensive ones (I have an Italian machine that cost a lot, but still works well after twenty years) to more reasonable electric ones where you put in the ice and rock salt. You can also really get back to basics (and get the kids involved!) with a hand-crank machine (just think of homemade peach ice cream on a summer afternoon . . .).

After you make the base, put it in a bowl, chill it in the refrigerator, and, when you're ready, churn it in the machine to harden it. Then freeze until you need it.

MY BASIC RECIPE

2 cups cream

2 cups milk

¾ cup sugar

8 egg yolks

1. Heat the cream, milk, and sugar in a saucepan; scald.
2. Place the egg yolks in a bowl; slowly add the scalded cream-milk mixture, whisking constantly (don't add it too quickly or you will scramble the eggs).
3. Pour the mixture into the saucepan and, with a flat-bottomed wooden spoon, stir till the mixture coats the spoon and is approximately 170°F. on an instant-read thermometer.
4. Remove the mixture immediately; strain and put in the refrigerator to cool. Everything can be done to this point a few days ahead.
5. Add flavors accordingly. (Never add more than 3 to 4 tablespoons of alcohol per quart of ice cream or it will be icy.)
6. Churn and freeze.

Butter Pecan Ice Cream

When I was a kid, we used to go out for ice cream cones with the whole family at least once a week during the summer, usually on Sunday. But the little ice cream parlor in my hometown was too small for all of us (four kids plus my mom and dad). So we kids would all squeal out what flavors we wanted and my dad would go in to get them. I don't think he could handle the confusion, because he always came back with six strawberry ice cream cones, which must have been his favorite flavor! I was always dreaming of butter pecan ice cream . . . So here it is!

3/4 cup packed light brown sugar

5 tablespoons unsalted butter

2 tablespoons water

1/2 vanilla bean, split and scraped

2 cups heavy cream

2 cups milk

7 egg yolks

3/4 cup pecan halves

In a saucepan over medium-high heat, combine the brown sugar, 4 tablespoons of the butter, the water, and the vanilla bean and simmer, stirring, for 30 seconds. Add the cream and milk and mix well. Heat until bubbles form around the edges.

In another saucepan, whisk the egg yolks. Add the scalded cream mixture to the egg yolks very slowly, whisking constantly. When all of it has been added, set the saucepan over medium heat and, *stirring constantly* with a flat-bottomed wooden spoon, cook until the mixture coats the spoon or until an instant-read thermometer registers 170°F. *Do not let this mixture boil!* Immediately remove it from the heat. Strain the custard into a bowl and whisk immediately to cool. Refrigerate until cold.

Preheat the oven to 350°F. While the ice cream base is chilling, melt the remaining 1 tablespoon butter. Toss with the pecans and place on a baking sheet. Bake until the pecans are light golden and smell nutty, 5 to 7 minutes. Chop the pecans coarsely and let cool.

Pour the chilled ice cream base into an ice cream maker and freeze according to the manufacturer's instructions. During the last 2 minutes of the churn cycle, add the pecans.

MAKES I GENEROUS QUART

Chestnut Honey Ice Cream with Riesling Poached Fruit

This delicious dessert calls for a late harvest dessert wine; that's one made with grapes that have been left on the vine longer than usual. Producing this distinctive wine that I call "liquid gold" also combines luck, poetry, boldness, commitment, skill, and a beneficial fungus called *botrytis cinerea*. You don't need a Château d'Yquem for this recipe, just a good-quality late-harvest Riesling. For this dessert, it will create poetry enough. Chestnut honey is made in Italy from chestnut flowers. It has a much more pronounced honey flavor. If chestnut honey is unavailable, substitute your favorite honey.

ICE CREAM

2 cups heavy cream

²/₃ cup milk

1 vanilla bean, split and scraped

6 egg yolks

3 tablespoons sugar

¹/₄ cup chestnut honey

COMPOTE

3 cups late harvest riesling

3 tablespoons chestnut or any
    honey

4 whole cloves

1 4-inch strip lemon zest, white
    pith removed

2 Bosc pears, peeled, halved, cored,
    and cut into eighths

¹/₂ cup dried figs (about 2¹/₂ ounces)

¹/₂ cup dried apricots (about
    2¹/₂ ounces)

¹/₂ cup golden raisins (about
    2¹/₂ ounces)

¹/₂ cup pitted dried plums or
    prunes (about 2¹/₂ ounces)

Make the ice cream: In a large saucepan, scald the cream, milk, and vanilla bean and seeds. Remove from the heat, cover, and let the flavor of the vanilla bean infuse for 30 minutes. In a large bowl, beat the egg yolks with the sugar and honey for a few minutes until the sugar has dissolved. Set aside.

Reheat the cream to scalding. Pour about one-quarter of the hot cream into the egg yolks mixture, whisking constantly. Pour the mixture into the saucepan and whisk together with the remaining cream. Cook over low heat, stirring constantly with a flat-bottomed wooden spoon, until the mixture thickens enough to coat the back of the spoon. Strain through a fine-mesh strainer into a bowl. Whisk a few times to cool slightly, then refrigerate until completely chilled.

Pour the chilled mixture into an ice cream maker and freeze according to the manufacturer's instructions.

Make the compote: Place the wine, honey, cloves, and lemon zest in a saucepan over high heat. Bring to a boil, then reduce the heat to low. Add the pears and simmer until tender, 10 to 15 minutes. Using a slotted spoon, transfer the pears to a bowl. Discard the cloves and lemon zest. Add the figs, apricots, raisins, and prunes and simmer until the fruit is tender, about 10 minutes and the wine is reduced by half. Add the pears and simmer until warm, 1 to 2 minutes.

To serve, warm the fruit compote. Scoop the ice cream into bowls and spoon the fruit compote on top.

SERVES 6

SWEETER THAN WINE

The one rule about drinking wine with dessert is this: The dessert cannot be sweeter than the wine. If it is, the wine will taste a bit sour.

A good rule of thumb for determining how cold a dessert wine should be is, the sweeter the wine, the cooler the temperature. You'll get the right temperature by chilling your Sauternes or sweet champagne for four to five hours in the refrigerator prior to serving.

Bellinis

Happily, my birthday falls around the time white peaches come into season. So it seems right to toast another year with these luscious drinks that combine white peaches and sparkling wine. Prosecco, a naturally sparkling wine from northern Italy, should be available at your local wine shop; if not, use sparkling wine or champagne. A wonderful opener for Saturday morning breakfast or Sunday brunch, they can be served with Baked Eggs with Summer Vegetables (page 74) and Jalapeño-Jack Scones with Chive Butter (page 77).

> 2 pounds ripe white peaches
> Salt
> 1 teaspoon lemon juice
> 1 bottle Prosecco

Bring a pot of water to a boil. Boil the peaches for 20 seconds. Remove immediately and let cool. Peel the peaches, cut in half, and discard the pit. Puree the peach flesh in the blender until smooth. Add a pinch of salt and the lemon juice, and stir together.

Mix 2 cups of the peach puree with the Prosecco. Pour into champagne glasses and serve immediately.

SERVES 6

"San Francisco has only one drawback. 'Tis hard to leave."

RUDYARD KIPLING

METRIC EQUIVALENCIES

Liquid and Dry Measure Equivalencies

CUSTOMARY	METRIC
1/4 teaspoon	1.25 milliliters
1/2 teaspoon	2.5 milliliters
1 teaspoon	5 milliliters
1 tablespoon	15 milliliters
1 fluid ounce	30 milliliters
1/4 cup	60 milliliters
1/3 cup	80 milliliters
1/2 cup	120 milliliters
1 cup	240 milliliters
1 pint (2 cups)	480 milliliters
1 quart (4 cups)	960 milliliters (.96 liter)
1 gallon (4 quarts)	3.84 liters
1 ounce (by weight)	28 grams
1/4 pound (4 ounces)	114 grams
1 pound (16 ounces)	454 grams
2.2 pounds	1 kilogram (1000 grams)

Oven-Temperature Equivalencies

DESCRIPTION	°FAHRENHEIT	°CELSIUS
Cool	200	90
Very slow	250	120
Slow	300–325	150–160
Moderately slow	325–350	160–180
Moderate	350–375	180–190
Moderately hot	375–400	190–200
Hot	400–450	200–230
Very hot	450–500	230–260

ACKNOWLEDGMENTS

A book and a television series is the sum of many parts. It is here that I hope to thank everyone who has played such a special part in my life for the last couple of years while I worked on this project, *Weir Cooking in the City.*

For her patience, dedication, and support, I would like to thank my editor, Sydny Miner, and the team at Simon and Schuster, especially Laura Holmes, Linda Dingler, Laura Lindgren, Mia Crowley, Jackie Seow, and Leah Wasielewski. Syd, you took my thoughts and recipes and formed them into this lovely book and, in the end, made me feel like it's mine. Thank you. And of course, a very special thanks to my dear friend and agent, Doe Coover. No one comes close!

This book wouldn't have been possible without my friend and loyal supporter, Penina. Your art is magic, and I thank you for gracing the pages of my cookbook yet again with your wonderful photographs. Thanks to Sara Slavin for her exquisite propping and quick wit, and to Amy Nathan, who styled my book as though it were her own.

Barbara Ignatius is the unsung hero. For her superb writing, editing, and managing of this project, a big hug and thank you. There has never been a friend as loyal; a brilliance so true. I would also like to thank recipe testers Jean Tenanes (aka Mom), Barbara McGee, and Bruce Fielding. As always, you give one hundred percent and then some! Thanks to Judy Witts Francini for her recipes again and again. You are one of the most generous people I know. To my pal Tim McDonald for his wine savvy and expertise. Thank you to Tracey McKeown for getting me through the day-to-day. I would also like to thank a few friends who keep me on track with their love and support—Gary Danko, Bibby Gignilliat, Kraemer Winslow, Charlotte Robinson, Linda Pratt, and, of course, Francisco Ubaldo.

And I wouldn't even be here without John, Jean, Johnny, Nancy, Jinny, Gianna, Liz, Niki, Beth, Sara, Cory, Becky, David, and Jack. When times are tough, I call. When times are good, I call. Thanks for always being there.

Now let's talk about indebtedness. Tina Salter is absolutely the best producer one could ever dream of! We talked so many years ago about this television project. I'm not sure I ever imagined we would be doing this together but, Tina, you believed in me and the project. Your dedication, hard work, kindness, and utmost support have turned *Weir Cooking in the City* into an incredibly pleasurable journey. I thank my lucky stars every single day. To Deanne Hamilton, who said "Yes!" from the beginning, supported me, and pursued it to the end. I have loved working with you, Deanne. A big thanks to Monica Caston, director, for her quick eye and gentle coaching. Thanks to Linda Giannecchini, assistant director, for her calm guidance. I am also grateful to Danny McGuire, who oversees us all and cheers me on every day. To Elizabeth Pepin, who not only tells me what to wear but also teaches me to drive my fire engine–red Bajaj. To Christine Swett for her kindness, discerning eye, and attention to every detail. To Laura Batistich for her calm efficiency and creative suggestions. To Brian Erskine for making sure the food looked exactly like mine. To Bruce Fielding, whose cooking skills are second to none, thank you. To Jolee Hoyt for gently cracking the whip and keeping us on budget! To Brad Gunnell: I knew we could do it! Our perseverance has paid off! Thanks to both you and Don Derheim for believing in the project! And to Stephanie Green, who followed up with the details. Thanks to Ron Haake for his incredible kitchen design and to my friend Celia Tejada for her attention to detail. A special thanks to my friend and art director, Bernie Schimbke; this is our third series together, Bernie, and I am thrilled you are part of the team. Thanks to Lorraine Battle for her attention to detail and hard work behind the scenes. Thanks to Jenny Zielon for gracing my face with her gentle touch.

But the truth of the matter is, this show wouldn't be possible without so many wonderful friends and funders for the show. Thanks to the team at Sur La Table—Renee and Carl Behnke, Doralece Dullaghan, Susanna Linse, and Gayle Novacek. To everyone at Turning Leaf Coastal Reserve and EJ Gallo—Lou Paskalis, Stephanie Gallo, Sue McClelland, Tim McDonald, and Jennifer Dadesho. And to everyone at Libbey

Glass—Jaci Volles, Elizabeth Geronimo, and Greg Pax. A big thanks to everyone at Thai Kitchen, Seth Jacobson, Jerry Maynard, and John Wright.

And finally, I know that there are so many other people who have played a very special part in either the book or the TV series and I want to thank you all from my heart for your creativity, dedication, and support. The world is a better place for your presence and so is *Weir Cooking in the City.*

—*Joanne Weir*

■　■　■

Gathering the ingredients and equipment together for a recipe is the first step toward making a great dish. We refer to the process as assembling the *mise en place,* or getting the "things in place." That is precisely where we are as I write this. We are in the process of gathering together butchers and bakers, fishmongers and grocery stores, dairy girls and farmers to supply the food. We are gathering appliance companies, kitchen equipment manufacturers, knife makers, and those companies that design and build all the little tools that we rely on to make our lives easier. We are talking to furniture companies, potters, rug makers, and artists to decorate the new kitchen as it takes shape in the studio. Then there are the clothing designers for wardrobe, transport details, and so many other ingredients still to be found.

Preparing the ingredients for the recipe of *Weir Cooking in the City* is a huge project. But the most important part of the process is gathering together talented individuals and molding them into a cohesive team to showcase Joanne's talents. They are the camera operators, floor directors, sound, video, and technical crew who prepare and record the tape; they are the editors who finesse the story and the operations staff who organize them. They are the chefs who garnish the plate.

Some of those individuals are already on board and can be named. Others are yet to sign on, but they are just as important. We can't acknowledge them by name here, but their influence is apparent in the final shows.

Thank you to you all! You are a part of the recipe and we are looking forward to a great meal. . . .

Director: Monica Caston; Assistant Director: Linda Giannecchini; Floor Directors: Randy Brase, Margaret Clarke, and Jean Tuckerman; Camera Operators: Harry Betancourt, Bill Bishop, Greg King, Greg Overton, and Rick Santangelo; Lighting Directors: Greg King and Jim McKee; Audio: Birrell Walsh and Helen Silvani; Engineering Supervisor and Video Engineer: Eric Shackelford; Technical Director: John Andreini; Videotape Operator: Jon Morris; Editor: Kirk Goldberg; Manager, TV Production Operations: Frank Carfi ; and Operations Coordinator: Kim McCalla; Manager, Engineering Operations: Ernie Neumann; Graphic Design: Caroline Hendriks and Janet Raugust; Publicity: Victoria Shelton; Program Distribution: Regina Eichner Eisenberg; Web Design: Wendy Goodfriend; Music: John Lawrence, Power of 2 Music.

Kitchen Manager: Brian Erskine; Kitchen Staff: Gayle Gonzales, Rebecca Klus, Jacqueline Schwartz, and Jesus Rodriguez; and Production Support: Erika Kennedy, Holly Malander, Oscar Robles, Jason Mecum, Angel Sheef, and Doug Whitlow.

Locations: Bryan's Meats, Boulangerie Bay Bread, Swan Oyster Depot, Blue and Gold Ferry, Town of Tiburon, City of Pacifica, Mario's Bohemian Cigar Store, Gary Danko's, Sur La Table, El Metate, The Cayenne, South Beach Harbor, Waxen Moon Candles, La Palma Mexicatessen, The Ferry Plaza Farmers' Market, Bombay Bazaar, Truly Mediterranean, The Pasta Shop, Tartine, and Danilo Bakery.

Wardrobe Provided by: Isda & Co and Margaret O'Leary

Bajaj Scooter Provided by: San Francisco Scooter Centre and Bajaj USA

Appliances Provided by: Dacor

Food and Wine Provided by:

Andronico's Market

Bi-Rite

Cowgirl Creamery

Diamond of California

Freixenet USA

GreenLeaf Produce

Maple Leaf Farms

McEvoy Organic Extra-Virgin Olive Oil

Peet's Coffee and Tea

Petaluma Poultry

Smart & Final

Straus Family Creamery

The Fresh Fish Company

Vanilla, Saffron Imports

Special Thanks to:

All-Clad Cookware

Chinook Planks Seattle

Cuisinart

Cuisipro

Emile Henry

Estate Wines, Ltd.

Flama U.S.A.

Ironwood

Kohler

Le Creuset

MAC Knife, Inc.

Microplane

Nespresso

Oscartielle

OXO Good Grips

Pottery Barn

Paige Poulos Communications

Screwpull

Staub USA

The Glad Products Company

The Wine Hardware Store

Vita-Mix Corporation

West Marine

Wines.com

WÜSTHOF-Trident of America, Inc.

—*Tina Salter*